AROMAT

With Properties of Essential Oils and procedures of Spa and Different types of Massage

Dr. Rajeev Sharma
M.D., D.Lit.

MANOJ PUBLICATIONS

Publishers :

Manoj Publications
761, Main Road, Burari, Delhi-110084
Ph: 27611116, 27611349, Fax : 27611546
Mobile : 9868112194
E-mail : *manojpublications@vsnl.net*
Website : *www.manojpublications.com*

Showroom :

Manoj Publications
1583-84, Dariba Kalan, Chandani Chowk,
Delhi-110006
Ph. : 23262174, 23268216, Mob. : 9818753569

Warnings : This books is not intended as an alternative to personel, professional medical advice. The reader should consult a physician in all matters relating to health, and particularly in respect of any symptoms which may require diagnosis or medical attention. While the advice and information are believed to be accurate and true at the time of going to press, neither the author nor the publisher can accept any legal responsibility or liaility for any errors or omissions that may be made.

ISBN : 81-310-0095-8

First Edition : 2005

Price : 80/-

Printers :

Adarsh Printers
Naveen Shahdara, Delhi-110032

Aromatherapy : *Dr. Rajeev Sharma*

A Brief about the Author

Dr. Rajeev Sharma is an eminent consultant of Homeopathy, Yoga, Naturopathy and Alternative Medicine in India. He has written more than 150 books in Hindi and English and around one thousand articles which have been published in various newspapers and magazines. He is also an Editorial Board Member of the prestigious *Asian Homeopathic Journal* besides many other newspapers and magazines.

Dr. Rajeev Sharma has written books on ayurveda, allopathy, homoeopathy, yoga, naturopathy, acupressure, magnetotherapy, reiki, water-therapy, massage and aromatherapy etc.

The books written by Dr. Rajeev Sharma are published by renowned publishers of India. Besides this he is doing editing and translation also. He is content provider to many magazines.

Dr. Rajeev Sharma has written books on all major ailments like diabetes, hypertension, obesity, stomach and respiratory disorders, E.N.T. disorders, female disorders, UTI disorders, paediatric problems, headache, stress and other mental problems and sexual disorders etc.

Dr. Rajeev Sharma is Medical Advisor to Ralson Remedies (a homoeopathic manufacturer), and Dixit Pharmacy (Ayurvedic Manufacturer), Medical Examiner at the LIC and Medical Officer in U.P. Govt. He has received several awards for his outstanding achievements. He has been awarded the *Best Author prize in Hindi* by the Ministry of Health and Family Welfare, Government of India and *Sarjana Puraskar by U.P. Hindi Sansthan,* Lucknow.

He has delivered talks on All India Radio and lectures on Alternative Medicine in various Government and Non-government Organisations. He has written Advt. Scripts for the products of several companies.

He is working as Vastu Fengshui Consultant, Educational Consultant and Marriage and Behaviour Counsellor too.

He also delivered lectures and provide literature on Persosnality Development and Life Style Management also to the MNC's.

He has established an institute through which you can get certificates by correspondence in Acupressure, Massage, Yoga, Water Therapy, Diet Therapy, Naturopathy, Colour Therapy and Reiki besides other paramedical courses.

Dr. Rajeev Sharma is also a social activist. He has worked a lot against Addiction and prevention of AIDS. Now-a-days, he is working to check the population growth of India with an NGO called 'Nav Chetna Manch'. He has worked for pollution control and human rights too and has received the World Human Rights Promotion Award. His name has been published in *LIMCA BOOK OF RECORDS*. He has developed two websites too :

www.newkamasutra.com : A site of love, romance and sex.
www.indiaalive.net : Patriotic site (Future planning)

He is a person of creative mind.

PREFACE

Good smell can ignite us, while bad smell can upset our mood. The science of good smells is aromatherapy.

The aroma enter our nose and connects with cilia, the fine hair inside the nose lining. The receptors in the cilia are linked to the olfactory bulb which is at the end of the smell tract. The end of the tract is in turn connected to the brain itself. Smells are converted by cilia into electrical impulses that are transmitted to the brain through olfactory system.

All the impluses reach the limbic system. Limbic system is that part of the brain which is associated with our moods, emotions, memory and learning. All the smells that reaches the limbic system has a direct chemical effect on our moods.

For example, a whiff of jasmine increases beta waves in the brain and this wave is associated with an increased agile and alert state. Swelling lavender increases alpha waves in the brain and it is this wave that helps us to relax.

The moleculor sizes of essential oils are very tiny and they can easily penetrate through the skin and get into the blood stream. It takes between a few seconds to two hours for the essential oils to enter the skin and within four hours the toxins get out of the body through urine, perspiration and excreta.

Aroma oils work like magic for stress related problems, psychosomatic disorders, skin infections, hair loss, inflammations, pains arising from muscular or skeletal disorders to name some of the applications.

There are different way of using essential oils like rubbing, bath, massage, inhalation, should he used in lesser quantity by mixing in proper carrier oils and under guidance of some expert.

If you have any query, you can write to me with a reply envelope but please do not come without prior appointment.

With thanks and regards.

Dr. Rajeev Sharma

Srijan : AAROGYA JYOTI®,

WINDSOR, PALM-11/03,

SHIPRA SUN CITY

Indirapuram, Ghaziabad (U.P.)

Email : sharmarajeev108@rediffmail.com

drrajeev108@newkamasutra.com

CONTENTS

Aromatherapy is already slowly getting into the mainstream. In Japan, engineers are incorporating aroma systems into new buildings. In one such application, the scent of lavender and rosemary is pumped into the customer area to calm down the waiting customers, while the perfumes from lemon and eucalyptus are used in the bank teller counters to keep the staff alert.

1

ORIGIN OF AROMATHERAPY

The oldest use of aroma oils is known to be as old as 6000 years back when Egyptian physician, Imhotep, the then God of Medicine and Healing recommended fragrant oils for bathing and massaging. In 4,500 B.C. Egyptians used myrrh and cedar wood oils for embalming their dead and 6,500 years later the preserved mummies prove the fact discovered by the modern researchers that the cedar wood contains natural fixative and strong anti-bacterial and anti-septic properties.

Hippocrates, the Greek father of Medicine, recommended regular aroma therapy baths and scented massages. This is what he effectively used to ward off plague from Athens.

Romans utilised essential oils for pleasure and to cure pain and also for their popular perfumed baths and massages. Emperor New being indulgent in orgies, feasts and fragrances employed rose frequently to cure his headaches, indigestion and to maintain his high spirits while enjoying amusements.

During the great plague in London in 1665, people burnt bundles of lavender, cedar wood and cypress in the streets and carried posies of the same plants as their only defence to combat infectious diseases.

Aroma therapy received a wider acceptance in the early 20th Century. In 1930s Rene-Maurice-Gatte Fosse, a French chemist, dipped his burnt hand in lavender oil. To his surprise the wound healed very quickly without any infection or scarring. He did considerable research on various oils and their therapeutic and psychotherapeutic properties.

Dr Jean Volnet, French army surgeon extensively used essential oils in World War II. It was Madame Morquerite Murry who gave the holistic approach to aroma oils by experimenting with them for individual problems.

Today, research has proved the multiple use of aroma oils. Medical research in the recent years has uncovered the fact that the odours we smell have a significant impact on the way we feel. Smells act directly on the brain like a drug according to scientific research. For instance smelling lavender increases alpha wave frequence in the back of the head and this state is associated with relaxation.

Essential oils like spiritual healing (Reiki, Pranic, Magnified), homeopathic, herbal and flower remedies have a life force that vibrates within the body and the benefit exerted is too subtle to evaluate.

❑❑

2

HOW DOES AROMA OILS WORK?

Dr Alan Huch, a neurologist, psychiatrist and also the director of Smell and Taste Research Centre in Chicago says, "Smell acts directly on the brain, like a drug". Our nose has the capacity to distinguish 1,00,000 different smells, many of which, affect us without our knowing about the same.

Essential oils are safe to use

The aroma enters our nose and connects with cilia, the fine hair inside the nose lining. The receptors in the cilia are linked to the olfactory bulb which is at the end of the smell tract. The end of the tract is in turn connected to the brain itself. Smells are converted by cilia into electrical impulses that are transmitted to the brain through olfactory system. All the impulses reach the limbic system. Limbic system is that part of the brain which is associated with our moods, emotions, memory and learning. All the smell that reaches the limbic system has a direct chemical effect on our moods.

For example, smelling lavender increses alpha waves in the brain and it is this wave that helps us to relax. A whiff of jasmine increases beta waves in the brain and this wave is associated with an increased agile and alert state.

Limbic system is also a storehouse of millions of remembered smells. That is why the mere fragrance of haystack takes us back to childhood.

The molecular sizes of the essential oils are very tiny and they can easily penetrate through the skin and get into the blood stream. It takes anything between a few seconds to two hours for the essential oils to enter the skin and within 4 hours the toxins get out of the body through urine, perspiration and excreta.

Aroma oils work like magic for stress-related problems, psychosomatic disorders, skin infections, hair loss, inflammations, pains arising from muscular or skeletal disorders to name some of the application. Actually essential oils have innumerable applications.

In Bristol, lavender oil was used on 28 patients who had undergone by-pass surgery. 24 of them reported reduced breathing rates, lower blood pressure and anxiety levels.

In Paris, in 1985, 28 women were given treatment for thrush using essential oils. After 90 days the clinical examination showed that 21 of them had been cured completely.

Essential oils are safe to use. The only caution being they should never be used directly because some oils may irritate sensitive skin or cause photo-sensitivity. They should be blended in adequate proportion with the carrier oils. A patch test is necessary to rule out any reactions.

❑❑

3

HOW TO USE AROMA OILS

Essential oils can be used in a variety of ways at home and place of work. Some of the common ways are:

Inhalation : Add 2-3 drops of essential oil depending on which oil you have selected to the hot boiling water and inhale the steam by covering your head with a towel to stop the steam from escaping. Steaming also helps to open the pores of the skin and thus more oil is absorbed giving the additional benefit of a facial.

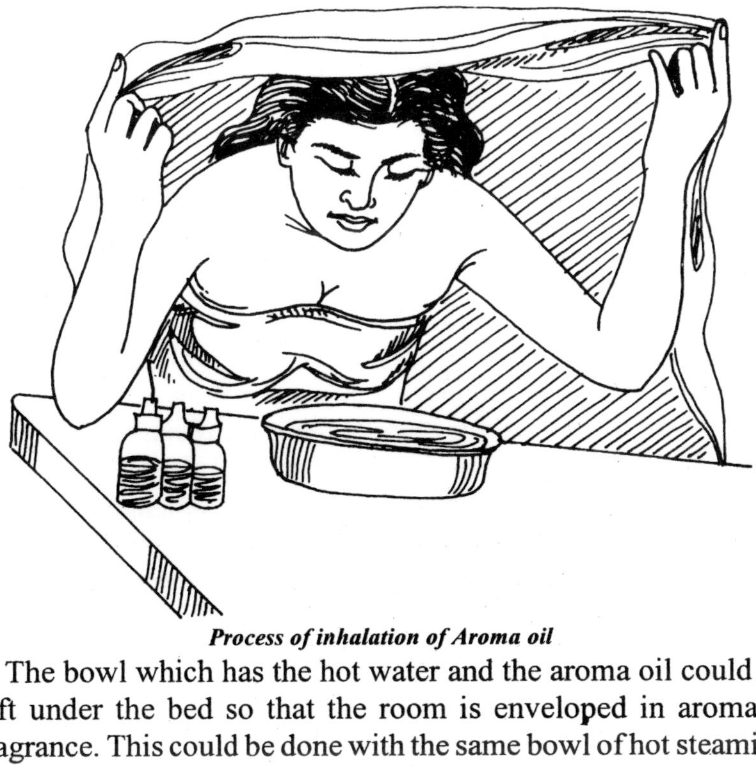

Process of inhalation of Aroma oil

The bowl which has the hot water and the aroma oil could be left under the bed so that the room is enveloped in aromatic fragrance. This could be done with the same bowl of hot steaming water and essential oil which had been used earlier for inhalation. A drop or two sprinkled on a handkerchief can give a lasting benefit of the aroma oil. For a very peaceful and relaxed sleep one or two drops of essential oils on a tissue kept inside the pillow or cushion could be used.

Diffusers and Vapourisers : Diffusers are generally made of ceramic or clay. The diffusers has a cave like opening to house small candles or earthen oil lamps and the top is shaped like a curved cup to hold a little water and few drops of aroma oil. Fill the top cup with water, add a few drops of essential oils depending on the oil chosen then light the candle or the lamp. For the oil lamp to last for a long duration, add castor oil to the earthen lamp because castor oil burns for a very long time as compared to the other oils used to light a lamp. Once the water and oil heat up, evaporation takes place and the whole atmosphere is filled with the aromatic scent. The process of evaporation continues for nearly five to six hours. This is ideal for presenting a conducive ambience during a gathering or even in bedrooms, hotels, living-rooms, etc., and anywhere where scented air is required. One can get instant relief from pain, a relaxed and positive feeling prevails when the right oil is used. One needs to be careful in choosing the right essential oil.

Vaporisers are the insect repellents used normally in the form of mats or other types of vaporisers kept for repelling insects. One could reuse the used mats by adding 2-3 drops of essential oil of your own choice and keeping them lit (electrically). Slowly the smell will get released and the area would be filled with soothing aroma. Lemon or rosemary are beneficial for offices, lavender for bedroom, antiseptic tea-tree for disinfecting a sick room and citronella for repelling the insects.

Massage : The most common form of treatment is massage because the dual benefits of touch therapy and scent therapy are simultaneously enjoyed. Massage improves the circulation of the blood, tones the muscles, detoxify toxins, releases trapped energy from tense muscles. The fragnance triggers a sense of pleasure and well being. The penetration of essential oil through the skin during massages is high. Generally carrier oils like sunflower, coconut, olive, sweet almond, sesame and vegetable oils are mixed with aroma oils. The aroma oils should not be used for massages directly without dilution. About 10 drops or 1 teaspoon of essential oil can be mixed to about 30 ml of carrier oil. This makes a very rejuvenating massage oil.

Baths : This is an easy way to relax using essential oils. Add the selected oil to your bathtub, stir the water well and spend 20 minutes in the tub. The aroma oil enters the body through the skin to give lasting benefits. Just a few drops are required to be added to the bathtub. The essential oils can also be added to a bucket of water instead of a bathtub. Mix the oil in the water properly, as some of the aroma oils are insoluble in water.

Foot Bath : You can immerse your feet in a bowl of lukewarm water to which 2-3 drops of essential oil is added. This is a very refreshing experience after a hard days work and if you have sweaty and smelly feet then too this foot bath is very profitable.

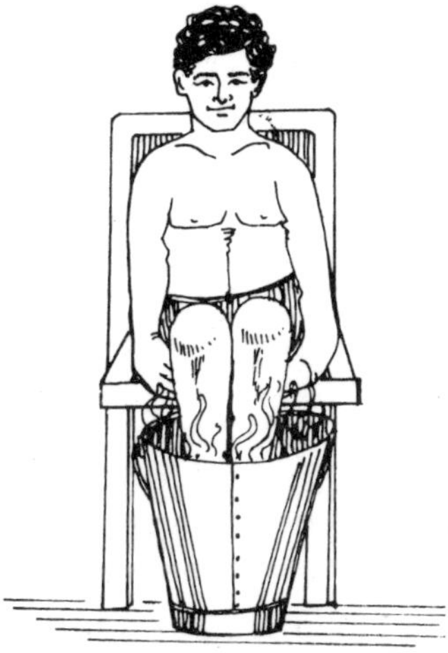

Hot Foot Bath

Pot Pourri : Pot pourri as the name suggests is a mixture of dried flowers, herbs, grass and seed pods. Few drops of essential oil added to the pot pourri and kept in a bowl would keep giving out aromatic fragrance for 4-6 weeks. Another more effective method would be to keep the pot pourri mixture after adding the essential oil in a closed container overnight so that the oil gets absorbed. The following morning the box can be kept open and the lingering aroma would fill the area.

Bed Time : Sprinkle 2-3 drops on the pillow cover or on a tissue that can be placed under the pillow or cushion cover and inhaled just before sleeping or while sleeping. This can be very useful in treating headaches, stress, tension and in boosting confidence. Some of the essential oils act as an aphrodisiac too.

Compresses : Both cold and hot compresses are profitable.

Add 2-3 drops of aroma oil to a bowl of hot (depending on how much of heat you can withstand) or warm water and dip a hand towel or piece of cotton to enable it to absorb the mixture then squeeze out the excess water and place the towel or cotton on the area to be treated. Leaving the compress on the area for 2 hours is quite beneficial. Oil like lavender is usually used. This provides relief when used over bruises, skin problems and pre menstrual syndromes. To make cold compress, add 6 cubes of ice to a bowl with 2-3 drops of essential oil. Dip a hand towel or a piece of cotton to absorb the mixture then squeeze out the excess water and place the towel or cotton on the area to be treated. Cold compress is highly helpful in treating burns, sore feet, hangover, sprains and headaches. After a facial the use of hot and cold compress alternately helps the skin to soothe.

Oral Intake : It is an accepted practice abroad to take essential oil orally as it is safe. However, care should be taken to take it only under the supervision or guidance of an experienced aroma therapy practitioner. Few oils can be taken internally in prescribed dosage for a particular problem like indigestion under the guidance of a qualified therapist only.

Room Sprays : There is a call for protecting the environment and this is becoming a prime concern world wide. Aerosols are being discouraged due to their ozone depleting properties. Essential oils are natural and hence they could be used liberally to deodorise a room, freshen and scent your bathroom, living-room, bedroom, dining-room, office cabin, etc. Merely add 10-12 drops of aroma oil to half a litre of water and spray the mixture with the help of a spray bottle. Oils like lavender, lemon, peppermint, pint and rosemary are best for this application. Cupboards, wardrobes can also be disinfected. If a room smells of dampness or there are moulds in the hotel rooms, houses, offices of factories and shops the essential oil along with water can be sprayed.

Beauty Treatment : Aroma oils have been used as an application for the skin from times immemorial. As they are highly soothing in treating and enhancing the natural beauty of the skin they can be safely incorporated in facials, massage, manicures, pedicures, scalp treatment, hair wash, hair treatment along with other creams and oils. Rose, chamomile, lemon, lavender, geranium, sandalwood are some good oils for facials irrespective of the fact that beauty treatment is given to normal, mature, dry, oily, sensitive or problem skin. Either one of these or a combination of two of them could be used. The carrier oils that are helpful in a beauty treatment are sweet almond, wheat germ, peach kernel, apricot kernel and sunflowers. Steam facials with essential oils are also rejuvenating and help in improving the skin texture.

Beauty care by Aroma oils

Insect Repellents : Essential oils are excellent fragrant dispenser and non toxic insecticides. Just 2-3 drops of essential oil can be used on pillow covers, mattresses or used mosquito mats (this can be electrically reused) or applied to the exposed skin after blending with carrier oil before going to bed to repel insects. Lemongrass is best for flying insects, tea-tree for ants and fleas, thyme for crawling pests, camphor for moths and citronella for mosquitoes. Even delicate plants (both indoor and outdoor) can be protected from insects by spraying the above essential oils to the roots of the plant.

Miscellaneous Uses : Aroma oil can be added to the water used for cleaning the house. It can be used to wipe the kitchen counter, platform, dining tables, babies' nappies for disinfecting purpose and also to wash the baths and toilets.

Aroma oils have versatile applications and innumerable benefits and can be made a part of our daily routine.

❑ ❑

4

CARRIER OILS

Carrier oils or base oils are vegetable, nut or seed oils. Many of these carrier oils also have therapeutic properties. Vegetable oils are extracted from the seeds of the plants. Vegetable oils contain a good amount of proteins nutrients and energy. They enable the body to produce heat and lubrication.

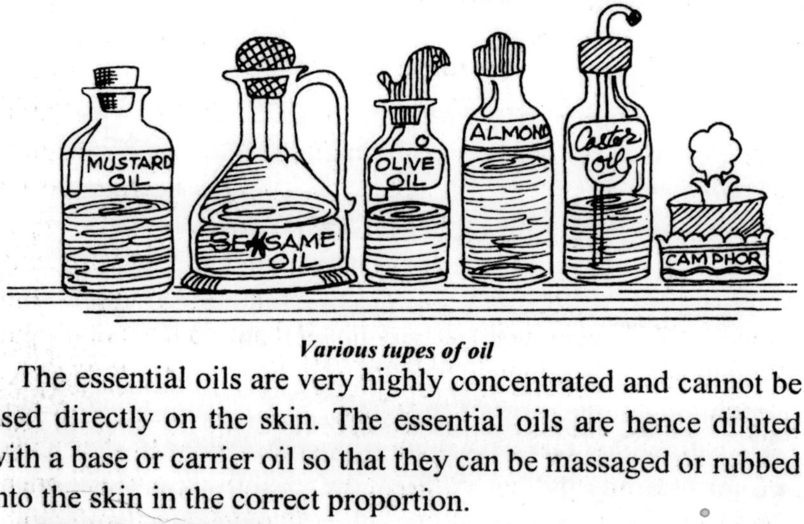

Various tupes of oil

The essential oils are very highly concentrated and cannot be used directly on the skin. The essential oils are hence diluted with a base or carrier oil so that they can be massaged or rubbed into the skin in the correct proportion.

Almond oil (Sweet)

Colour	:	very pale yellow
Extracted	:	from the kernel
Contains	:	glycosides, minerals, vitamins and proteins
Uses	:	good for skin, helps relieve itching, soreness, dryness and inflammation
Base oil	:	can be used as a base without dilution

Apricot kernel oil

Colour	:	pale yellow
Extracted	:	from the kernel
Contains	:	minerals, vitamins
Uses	:	all types of skin, particularly for prematured aged, sensitive, inflammed and dry skin
Base oil	:	can be used as a base without dilution

Avocado pear oil

Colour	:	dark green
Extracted	:	from the fruit
Contains	:	vitamins, proteins, lecithin and fatty acids.
Uses	:	all types of skin especially dry and dehydrated skin, eczema
Base oil	:	to be used as an addition to a base oil in 10 % dilution

Carrot oil

Colour	:	orange
Contains	:	vitamins, minerals, and beta-carotene
Uses	:	premature aging, itching, dryness, psoriasis and eczema. Very rejuvenating by itself and reduces scarring
Base oil	:	to be used as an addition to a base oil in 10% dilution. Do not use undiluted directly on the skin.

Corn oil

Colour	:	pale yellow
Contains	:	minerals, vitamins and protein
Uses	:	soothing for all types of skin.
Base oil	:	can be used as a base oil

Evening Primrose

Colour	:	pale yellow
Contains	:	vitamins, minerals, and gamma linolenic acid
Uses	:	during pre menstrual tension, multiple sclerosis, menopause related tensions, heart diseases. Excellent while treating eczema and psoriasis. Helps prevent premature aging of skin
Base oil	:	use in 10 % dilution.

Grapeseed oil

Colour	:	nearly colourless or pale green

Contains	:	vitamins, minerals, and protein
Uses	:	for all types of skin
Base oil	:	can be used as base oil without dilution

Hazelnut oil

Colour	:	yellow
Extracted	:	from the kernel
Contains	:	vitamins, minerals, and protein
Uses	:	for all types of skin. It has a slight astringent action
Base oil	:	use with 10% dilution

Peanut oil

Colour	:	pale yellow
Contains	:	vitamins, minerals, and protein
Uses	:	for all types of skin
Base oil	:	can be used as base oil without dilution

Safflower oil

Colour	:	pale yellow
Contains	:	vitamins, minerals, and protein
Uses	:	for all types of skin
Base oil	:	can be used as base oil without dilution

Sesame oil

Colour	:	dark yellow
Contains	:	vitamins, minerals, protein, lecithin and amino acids
Uses	:	rheumatism, arthritis, psoriasis, eczema. Useful for all types of skin
Base oil	:	use with 10% dilution

Soyabean oil

Colour	:	pale yellow
Contains	:	vitamins, minerals, and protein
Uses	:	for all types of skin
Base oil	:	can be used as base oil without dilution

Sunflower oil

Colour	:	pale yellow
Contains	:	vitamins, minerals, and protein
Uses	:	for all types of skin
Base oil	:	can be used as base oil without dilution

❑❑

5

CHIEF ESSENTIAL OILS AND THEIR BENEFITS

Different essential oils work on different parts of body and help to cure several diseases. Here is a summary of some important essential oils:

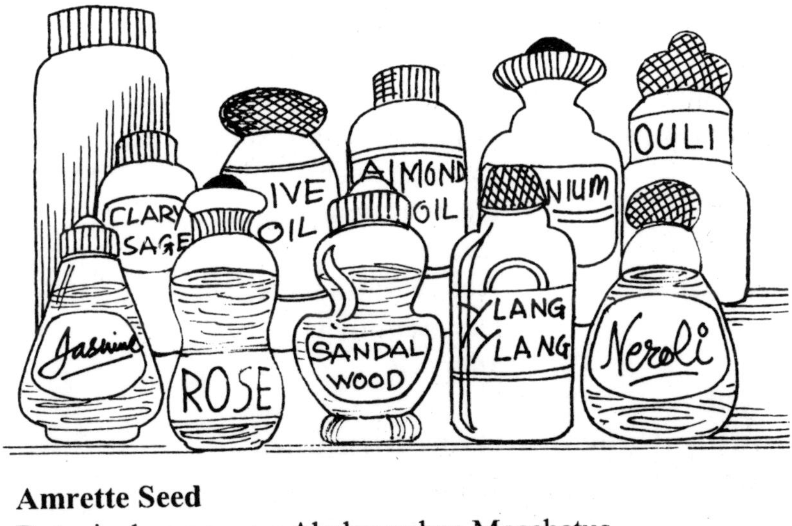

Amrette Seed

Botanical name	:	Abelmoschus Moschatus
Plant part	:	Seeds
Properties	:	Warmth-giving, relaxing, stimulating, calming
Quantity	:	2-3 drops
Application	:	Helpful in relieving anxiety, fatigue, depression or other stress related conditions, muscular aches, pains,

		cramps and poor circulation. Is an aphrodisiac. Excellent to freshen up tired and hurting feet
Precaution	:	Use in low dosage. Avoid very frequent massages or baths.

Aniseed

Botanical name	:	Pimpenella Anisum
Plant part	:	Seed pod
Properties	:	Warming, stimulating
Quantity	:	3-5 drops
Application	:	Helpful in treating coughs, bronchitis and catarrh.

Angelica

Botanical name	:	Angelica Archangelica
Plant part	:	Root, seed, fruit
Properties	:	Expectorant, digestive stimulant, relaxing
Quantity	:	2-3 drops
Application	:	Useful for colds, coughs, flu, muscular pains and aches, rheumatism. Helps in digestion. Also useful in healing smoker's cough.
Precaution	:	Avoid during pregnancy. Can cause photosensitivity, so avoid exposure to sun after use.

Basil

Botanical name	:	Ocimum Basilicum
Plant part	:	Leaves
Properties	:	Uplifting, refreshing
Quantity	:	2-3 drops
Application	:	Good for students and executives. Helps in relieving nervous tension, stress, mild anxiety, nausea, indigestion, flatulence, loss of appetite, temporarily relieves cough, sinusitis, flatulence, cold, fever, bronchitis, earaches, eases muscular

pains, spasm, rheumatic and arthritic pains. It also acts as an insect repellent

Precaution : Avoid during pregnancy.

Bergamot

Botanical name : Citrus Aurantium

Plant part : Peel of the fruit

Properties : Calming, refreshing, rejuvenating

Quantity : 3-5 drops

Application : Heals wounds and relieves ulcers, treats eczema, psoriasis (stress related) and PMT (Pre Menstrual Tension). Works as an appetiser. Beneficial in treating oily skin problems. Relieves respiratory infections *viz.* bronchitis, sore throat and tonsilitis, colic, flatulence and indigestion. Beneficial in treating anxiety, depression, mental and psychological disturbances. Acts as an antiseptic for urinary tract problem, cystitis. Effective in treating cold sores, chicken pox and shingles.

Precaution : Avoid using on sensitive skin as it can cause irritation. Avoid exposure to sun as it can increase skin's photosensitivity.

Black Pepper

Botanical name : Piper Nigrum

Plant part : Berry

Properties : Warming, strenthening

Quantity : 2-3 drops

Application : Helps in relieving muscular aches, pains, stiffness, fatigue. Useful in relieving physical and emotional problems. Gives temporary relief from arthritis, fibrosis, cold, flu, indigestion, respiratory infections, chills, catarrh. Helps in curing colic, flatulence, indigestion, heart burn

		and loss of appetite. Helps to maintain peripheral circulation, eases chilblains and tones muscles. Increases concentration and alertness.
Precaution	:	Use in moderation

Camphor

Botanical name	:	Cinnamomum Camphora
Plant part	:	Wood
Properties	:	Relieving
Quantity	:	2-3 drops
Application	:	Helps in treating coughs, colds, fevers, rheumatism, arthritis, constipation, insomnia, sprains, depression, acne and inflammed skin.
Precaution	:	Use in moderation.

Cardamom

Botanical name	:	Elettaria cardomumum
Plant part	:	Seeds
Properties	:	Warming
Quantity	:	2-3 drops
Application	:	Helps in relieving nausea, coughs, headaches, aches, digestion and it is a tonic
Precaution	:	Use in moderation.

Chamomile

Botanical name	:	Matricaria Chamomilia
Plant part	:	Flowers
Properties	:	Soothes
Quantity	:	3-5 drops
Application	:	Eases anxiety, anger and fear, helpful in treating insomnia, used for colitis, gastritis, diarrhoea, urinary tract infection, menopause and menstrual related problems. Relieves stress, depression and irritability related to PMT. Helps to relieve muscular pains, inflammation of arthritic joints and

		swollen joints. It is used in treating skin problems *viz.* psoriasis, dermatitis and eczema. Mild on children facing teething problem and earache. Soothes burns, blisters, inflammed wounds, broken capillaries. It can be used to lighten fair hair.
Precaution	:	Avoid during pregnancy.

Clove Bud

Botanical name	:	Syzygium Aromaticum
Plant part	:	Buds
Properties	:	Warming and soothing
Quantity	:	1-2 drops
Application	:	Relieves aches and pains (joints). Rheumatoid sprains, asthma, colds, flu, colic, dyspepsia, nausea, diarrhoea, toothache, ulcers, wounds, bronchitis, nervous tension, depression and stress. It is used as an effective antiseptic, and analgesic anti-bacterial. Useful as mosquito repellent and in fighting acne. Helps relieve athlete's foot and cuts.
Precaution	:	Use in low moderation. Avoid during pregnancy.

Cypress

Botanical name	:	Cupressus Sempervirens
Plant part	:	Needles, twigs
Properties	:	Refreshing, calming and strengthening
Quantity	:	2 drops
Application	:	An astringent to circulation, haemorhoids, varicose veins, cellulite; brings down external bleeding and excessive perspiration and heavy menstrual flow; useful in asthma, bronchitis, dry cough, cold and flu. Helps to heal swollen breasts.
Precaution	:	Avoid during pregnancy.

Clarysage

Botanical name	:	Salvia Sclarea
Plant part	:	Flowering tops
Properties	:	Euphoric, sensual, warming and relaxing
Quantity	:	2-5 drops
Application	:	Useful in dealing with anxiety, stress, tension and migraine, menstrual cramps and pains, PMT, muscular tension, excessive perspiration. Being warming and relaxing nourishes conversation. Brings down high blood pressure and excessive sebum. Reduces post natal depression and eases child birth by encouraging labour. Immune system gets strengthened. Eases asthma.
Precaution	:	Can cause drowsiness, avoid when under alcoholic effect. Avoid during pregnancy and also if one suffers from epilepsy.

Eucalyptus

Botanical name	:	Eucalptus Globulus
Plant part	:	Leaves, twigs
Properties	:	Cooling and clearing
Quantity	:	2-3 drops
Application	:	Clears stuffed nose and head. Acts as a decongestant; cures fever, cold. Relieves stress, fatigue, muscular pains, sprains, aches, rheumatism, headaches, sinusitis and mild respiratory infections. It is anti-inflammatory. Quite useful in treating wounds, burns, boils, abscesses, blisters, cold sore, shingles, blemishes, insect bites, anti-bacterial and is an insect repellent too.
Precaution	:	Can irritate skin. Keep away from children.

Fennel

Botanical name	:	Foeniculum Vulgare
Plant part	:	Seeds
Properties	:	Calming
Quantity	:	2-3 drops
Application	:	Useful in easing colic, constipation and digestion problems, fluid retention, cellulite, menstrual pain, PMT, menopause, nausea, flatulence and loss of appetite. Helps in fighting hangovers, increases flow of breast milk and relieves bronchitis. Cures kidney stones and relieves intestinal spasm. Has a mild diuretic and laxative effect.
Precaution	:	Avoid during pregnancy.

Frankincense

Botanical name	:	Olibanum Boswellia Carterii
Plant part	:	Gum resin
Properties	:	Fortifying, soothing
Quantity	:	3-5 drops
Application	:	Helps in meditation; slows and deepens breathing. Fortifies emotionally against nightmares, fear and grief. Balances and opens Crown chakra. It helps in healing ulcers and infected wounds. Treats dry, wrinkled, inflamed skin. It also cures coughs, laryngitis, asthma, catarrh and bronchitis. It reduces scar and promotes healing. Aids in maintaining supple skin by toning it.

Geranium

Botanical name	:	Pelargonium Graveolens
Plant part	:	Leaves, stalk, flower
Properties	:	Calming, balancing, relaxing, refreshing
Quantity	:	5-7 drops
Application	:	Helps to deal with nervous tension, anxiety, mood swings, depressin,

menopause problems, hot flushes, post natal depression, PMT, irregular menstruation. Treats swollen and painful breasts, fluid retention problems, emotional outbursts, irritability, throat infections. It cures colds, flu, neuralgia, sciatica, acne, bruises, burns, cuts, dermatitis, eczema, burns, cuts, mature skin and mouth ulcers. Normalises skin imbalances. Works as insect repellant, harmonises and calms. It also acts as an astringent and cleanser.

Ginger

Botanical name	:	Zingiber Officinale
Plant part	:	Root
Properties	:	Warming, stimulating
Quantity	:	2 drops
Application	:	Relieves colic, cramp, flatulence, nausea, travel sickness and indigestion. Cures migraine, coughs, congestion, common cold, catarrh, influenza, sore throat, sinusitis, arthritic pains, rheumatism, muscular aches, sprains and strains. Helps in blood circulation and aids memory. Heals bones and brings down temperature in fever also. Relieves morning sickness (if inhaled) in pregnancy and hangovers. Stimulates circulation, relaxes blood vessels and can also help ease angina.
Precaution	:	Use in low moderation. May irritate sensitive skin.

Juniper Berry

Botanical name	:	Juniperus Communis
Plant part	:	Berries
Properties	:	Uplifting, refreshing, relaxing
Quantity	:	2-3 drops

Application : Used to relieve stress, anxiety, pains of joints and rheumatic pain. Heals bruises, cramps, acne, colic, coughs, arthritis, menstrual pain, less menstrual flow, swollen and painful breasts (pre-menstrual). Deals with fluid retention, cellulite, obesity, poor circulation, haemorrohoids, loss of appetite. Tones the skin

Precaution : Avoid during pregnancy and if suffering from high blood pressure. Can irritate the kidneys if used in excess.

Lavender

Botanical name : Lavandula Angustifolia

Plant part : Flowers

Properties : Harmonising, soothing, balancing, refreshing, relaxing, calming

Quantity : 5-10 drops

Application : Aids in relieving irritability (in adults and children as well), anxiety, stress. Relieves muscular aches and pains, bites and stings. Cures colds, flu, insomnia, headache, minor burns and scalds. It is anti-fungal and anti-bacterial so it is very useful in treating wounds. It can be used directly to relieve pain of minor burns and scalds. It balances and harmonises the body.

Precaution : Avoid during early pregnancy.

Lemon

Botanical name : Citrus Limon

Plant part : Peel of fruit

Properties : Rejuvenating, enlivening, cooling, uplifting

Quantity : 3-6 drops

Application : Helps in healing bronchial problems, colds, flu, fever, sore throat, mouth ulcers, hormonal headaches, poor circulation, high blood pressure, wounds, stress, nervous tension and counteracts acidity. Aids in clearing freckels and to rid warts. Useful for students and executives. Helps in stopping hot flushes in menopause. It has an enliving and refreshing aroma and is an effective insect repellent too.

Precaution : Causes photo-sensitivity on sensitive skin. Avoid using when going out in sun as it may irritate sensitive skin.

Lemongrass

Botanical name : Cymbogen Citratus

Plant part : Grass

Properties : Tranquilizing, soothing calming, refreshing

Quantity : 1-3 drops

Application : Helps in relieving shock, grief, trauma, depression and stress. Helps to fight lethargy, irritability during PMT and menopause, insomnia, excitability in children, chronic diarrhoea triggered due to emotional reasons. Improves skin elasticity, thread veins, stretch marks and scars. It gives relief from headaches, sore throat and mild respiratory problems. Helps in opening the skin pores, treating oily skin, curing acne and relieves indigestion.

Precaution : Avoid during pregnancy. It can also irritate skin.

Marjoram

Botanical name : Origanum Marjorana

Plant part : Flowers, leaves

Properties : Calming, warming

Quantity : 3-5 drops

Application : Relieves anxiety, stress, high blood

pressure, arthritis, rheumatism, swollen joints, asthma, colds, flu, sinusitis. Cures migraines, stomach and menstrual cramps, indigestion, constipation and flatulence. Calming to the nervous system. Reduces sexual urges, heals bruises.

Precaution	:	Use in moderation. Avoid during pregnancy.

Neroli

Botanical name	:	Citus Aurantium
Plant part	:	Petals
Properties	:	Calming, soothing, refreshing
Quantity	:	1-3 drops
Application	:	Relieves mental lethargy, headaches, irritability caused due to menopause and PMT. It cures chronic diarrhoea due to emotional state and thread veins. Cures dryness, improves elasticity, sensitivity of skin and is also kind on mature skin. Calms excitable and restless children when used in baths before going to bed. Helps during shocks, trauma, grief and stress. Highly calming to those suffering from anxiety and fears. Helps lighten stretch marks and scars. Soothes palpitation, stress related problems and depression. Helps during pregnancy and labour.

Orange (Sweet)

Botanical name	:	Citrus Aurantium
Plant part	:	Peel
Properties	:	Calming, refreshing
Quantity	:	2-3 drops
Application	:	Effective in healing mouth ulcers, treats nervous tension, stress and anxiety. Gives

		relief from bronchial coughs, colds, flu and insomnia. Eases constipation and diarrhoea. It is very gentle on children brings down the fever.
Precaution	:	May increase skin photo-sensitivity. Avoid use before going out in the sun.

Palmarosa

Botanical name	:	Cymbopogon Martinii
Plant part	:	Grass
Properties	:	Clarifying, uplifting calming, refreshing
Quantity	:	4-5 drops
Application	:	Stimulates cell regeneration, circulation, appetite. It maintains a supple skin, removes scars, helpful in treating acne, dermatitis, balances sebum production, relieves indigestion, colds, flu, viruses and reduces fever.

Peppermint

Botanical name	:	Mentha piperita
Plant part	:	Leaves
Properties	:	Cooling, invigorating, comforting, refreshing, calming
Quantity	:	1-3 drops
Application	:	A decongestant which gives relief from asthma, colds, flu, fever, headaches, toothaches, sinusitis, nausea, travel sickness, stomach upsets and indigestion, hangover. Cools skin inflammation, burns and sunburns as it is very refreshing skin oil. Repels mosquitoes and rats.
Precaution	:	Use in moderation as it can irritate sensitive skin. Avoid during early pregnancy.

Patchouli

Botanical name	:	Pogostemon Cabin
Plant part	:	Leaves
Properties	:	Warming, exotic, calming, relaxing, enlivening

Quantity	:	2-4 drops
Application	:	Exotic aroma often used in perfumery. Emotionally enlivening, excites the senses. Helps in relieving anxiety, stress and, depression. Helps to heal chapped rough skin, wounds and sores. Being anti-inflammatory it helps cool inflammed skin. Effective in treating dandruff, scars. It is an antiseptic, astringent, anti-bacterial and insect repellent.
Precaution	:	Use in moderation as excess dose can cause sedation.

Petitgrain

Botanical name	:	Citrus Aurantium var Amara
Plant part	:	Leaves
Properties	:	Clarifying, soothing, uplifting
Quantity	:	4-5 drops
Application	:	Useful to relieve mental strain, restlessness, anxiety, tension, stress, flatulence, dyspepsia and constipation. Helps in stimulating digestion and poor momory. Brings down acne. Reduces excessive perspiration, treats greasy skin and hair. Helps to build up resistance to illness.

Pine

Botanical name	:	Pinus Sylvestris
Plant part	:	Needles
Properties	:	Invigorating, refreshing
Quantity	:	1-3 drops
Application	:	Relieves muscular aches, pains, Arthritis, rheumatism, poor circulation, asthma, bronchitis, coughs, catarrh, sinusitis, sore throats, colds, flu, nervous exhaustion, stress, fatigue, neuralgia, sciatica, poor

concentration. Heals cuts and abrasions, excessive perspiration. It is also an effective insect repellent.

Rose

Botanical name	:	Rose Centifoda damascena
Plant part	:	Leaves and flowers
Properties	:	Exciting, balancing
Quantity	:	1-4 drops
Application	:	Helps to ease depression, frigidity, nervous tension, headache and insomnia. Relieves asthma, shock, palpitations, poor circulation, dry coughs, nausea. Treats PMT, irregular or heavy menstruation, menstural pain, impotence, irritability. Hormonally balancing. Useful also for dry, chapped, aging skin and eczema.

Rosemary

Botanical name	:	Rosemarinus officinalis
Plant part	:	Leaves and flowers
Properties	:	Reviving, invigorating, focusing, refreshing
Quantity	:	2-4 drops
Application	:	Useful tonic for hair as it keeps dandruff at bay, clears lice, adds lustre to the hair. Useful in relieving stress, mental fatigue, anxiety, muscular aches and pains, rheumatism, arthritis, gout, sinusitis, migraine colds, flu, asthma, respiratory problem, poor circulation, fluid retention, cellulite, menstrual cramps, scanty flow during menstruation. Helps aid better concentration and clarity while studying.
Precaution	:	Avoid during pregnancy, if suffering from blood pressure or epilepsy.

Sandalwood

Botanical name	:	Santalum Album
Plant part	:	Wood

Properties : Strengthening, sedating, calming, relaxing
Quantity : 2-5 drops
Application : Helps to relieve nervous tension, depression, stress, anxiety, irritability, insomnia, dry coughs, sore throat, bronchitis, nausea, travel sickness. Heals inflamed, cracked, dry, chapped, mature, aging skin, acne, blemishes and scars. Acts as a deodoriser in case of excessive perspiration. Excites the senses. It is an effective insect repellent.

Tarragon

Botanical name : Artemisia Dracunculus
Plant part : Leaves
Properties : Calming
Quantity : 2-3 drops
Application : Useful to relieving stomach disorders, nervousness leading to butterflies or knots in the stomach, indigestion, flatulence, PMT, cramps, constipation. It is anti-spasmodic, antiseptic and slightly diruretic
Precaution : Avoid during pregnancy. Use in moderation.

Tea tree

Botanical name : Melaleuca Alternifolia
Plant part : Leaves, twigs
Properties : Soothing
Quantity : 2-5 drops
Application : Helpful in healing fungal and yeast infections, colds, influenza, cold sores, warts, burns, shock, bacterial and viral infections, stings, herpes, nappy rash and hysteria.

Thyme (White)

Botanical name : Thymus Vulgaris
Plant part : Leaves, flowers

Properties	:	Stimulating, invigorating
Quantity	:	2 drops
Application	:	Helpful in relieving tension, fatigue, anxiety, headaches, skin irritations, coughs, colds, rheumatic aches and pains. Useful insect repellent. It is a very good stimulant and expectorant.
Precaution	:	Avoid during pregnancy. Use in moderation.

Vetiver

Botanical name	:	Vetiveria Zizanoides
Plant part	:	Roots
Properties	:	Calming, balancing, grounding
Quantity	:	1-3 drops
Application	:	Helpful in relieving nervous tension, stress, muscular aches, pains, sprains, stiffness, arthritis, rheumatism, palpitation, congestion. Heals acne, blemishes, cuts and wound.

Ylang Ylang

Botanical name	:	Cananga Odorate
Plant part	:	Flowers
Properties	:	Balancing, relaxing
Quantity	:	2-3 drops
Application	:	Helps to relieve tension, uncontrolled anger, stress, anxiety, rapid heart rate, rapid breathing. Useful in high blood pressure, menopause, PMT, insomnia, impotence, frigidity, scalp conditioner. Useful for skin care.
Precaution	:	Avoid using after consuming alcohol or before driving. Use in moderation. It may cause headache and nausea when taken in excess.

❑❑

6

HOW TO SELECT ESSENTIAL OILS

The Best Aroma Oils:

Clarysage
Eucalyptus
Geranium
Lavender
Lemon
Peppermint
Petitgrain
Rosemary
Tea Tree
Ylang Ylang

Take necessary precautions before using Aroma oils

Male Favourites:

Basil
Bergamot
Eucalyptus
Frankincense
Lavender
Lemon
Petchouli
Pine
Sandalwood

Female Favourites:

- Bergamot
- Geranium
- Patchouli
- Peppermint
- Rose
- Lavender
- Neroli
- Clarysage
- Ylang Ylang

PRECAUTIONS BEFORE USING AROMA OILS

Skin Patch Test : To test aroma oil blended with carrier or base oils...

- ❑ Wash and dry the forearm thoroughly.
- ❑ Apply just a few drops of the blended aroma oil to moisten the area.
- ❑ Cover the area with a sterile gauze.
- ❑ Let it remain for 24 hours.
- ❑ If there is irritation then wash immediately.
- ❑ In case of irritation, you should not use this oil.

To test essential oil in its pure state...

- ❑ Wash and dry the forearm thoroughly with an unscented vegetable soap.
- ❑ Apply one drop of the aroma oil to the crook of the arm.
- ❑ Bend the arm so that it touches the shoulder for five minutes.
- ❑ Open and close once more.

If any irritation occurs wash immediately with water and soap or wipe carefully with a cotton ball soaked in milk and vegetable oil.

In case accidental poisoning occurs do the following:

Aroma oils being potent, safety precautions need to be followed with utmost care. Do not allow children to play with these oils and always store them away from the reach of children and other nonqualified users of essential oils.

IN EYES

In cases essential oil comes in contact with the eyes, do not rinse with water. But instead wipe the eye with a ball of cotton soaked in milk or vegetable oil. If irritation still persists wash the eyes with water poured from a jug, from a height of 3-5 inches for 15 minutes. Consult a doctor. It always helps to wash the eyes for 10 to 15 minutes than splashing it with running water.

TOXIC EFFECTS

Toxic effects can happen when the oil is not evenly spread out on the area and remains concentrated in one area in a large quantity. Even daily exposure to the same oil on a regular basis for a prolonged period can lead to toxicity. Symptoms that would follow a toxic reaction are fatigue, headaches, liver pain, liver enlargement, coughing and urine disturbances. This make it mandatory for the therapists using ventilated room and wash their hands thoroughly after handling the oils.

ALLERGIC EFFECTS

An allergic reaction to aroma oil would result in nausea, dizziness, sweating, stomach pain, mucous membrane, irritation and palpitation. These allergic reactions are temporary and would cease to exist as soon as the use of the essential oils is stopped.

The following precautions needs to be followed while dealing with essential oils having toxic rating.

The toxicity of the essential oils depends on the level of toxicity and concentration of the chemical compounds. All aroma oils need to be used as per instructions only and more so when handling those essential oils under toxic listing. Normally a toxic reaction occurs when the essential oil is used in excess or incorrectly. It is safer to use the aroma oils under proper guidance and instructions.

- Do not exceed the recommended dosage.
- If you feel uncomfortable even while using the recommended dosage reduce the dosage to half.
- Follow the skin patch test carefully.
- Avoid usage for a long period. The maximum administration time should not exceed 2 to 4 weeks. Leave a gap of 30 days before beginning to use again.
- Avoid use during pregnancy.
- Do not use if you are a nursing mother.
- Do not administer on infants, small children, frail or elderly people who have less resistance.

❑ ❑

7

SKIN CARE AND AROMATHERAPY

Skin not only covers and protects the body organs, it also excretes various toxins from the body through sweat and perspiration and, for the latter activity, skin pores serve as outlets for exit of toxins. If skin is healthy, good looking, soft, glazed, it is a boon for every one, whereas a rough skin denotes lack of sebacious oils that

Treat various skin disorders by using Aroma oils

feed and nutrient the skin. Essentail oils have excellent penetrative properties, apart from making useful moisturisers. But all essential oils and their preparations do not suit all types of skin. These oils can stimulate circulation of blood and the lymphatic system, cleanse the tissues which cause sluggishness to skin, treat various skin problems and general skin care.

Healthy skin is dependent on many factors, such as balanced diet, consisting of grain cereals, pulses, green vegetables, fresh seasonal fruits—rich in vitamins, minerals, dairy, poultry and sea products. In is pointed out that skin condition is also governed by various pshychic, emotional and sentimental factors. Environmental factors, pollutions in air & water, local weather conditions also play an important role in this regard.

TYPES OF SKIN

Certain weather conditions impact the skin greatly. For instance, skin can be dry in cold snowy and winter conditions, complexion usually darkens in summer, more oily during the period, in most conditions skin is more sticky and gives out unpleasant smell. It usually changes from puberty to menopause. So, one oil cannot be used for all the skins, rather it has to be changed in consonance with weather condition and the type of skin one has. Even oily skin can turn rough, cracked and dry and vice versa. Hence, choose an oil that suits best.

Following classifications will give an idea about the properties that a particular oil possess.

Oils for Dry Skin : Chamomile, Geranium, Hyssop, Lavender, Patchouli, Rose, Sandalwood, Ylang-Ylang.

Oils for Normal Skin : Chamomile (For Dry and Sensitive), Fennel (For Oily Skin), Geranium (For all types of skin) Lemon (For Oily Skin), Patchouli (For Dry Skin), Rose (For Dry and Sensitive Skin).

Oils for Oily Skin : Bergamost, Cedarwood, Cypress, Frankincense, Geranium, Juniper, Lavender, Lemon and Sage.

Oils for Sensitive Skin : Chamomile, Lavender, Neroli, Rose and Sandalwood.

In a few cases oils may be required to be blended, particularly when there is combination skin—in some cases skin may be normal from forehead to nose and chin, but dry in other body parts or it could be vicce versa also. In this case use oils for the oily skin on greasy areas and use suitable oils for normal skin on the rest of the area of face.

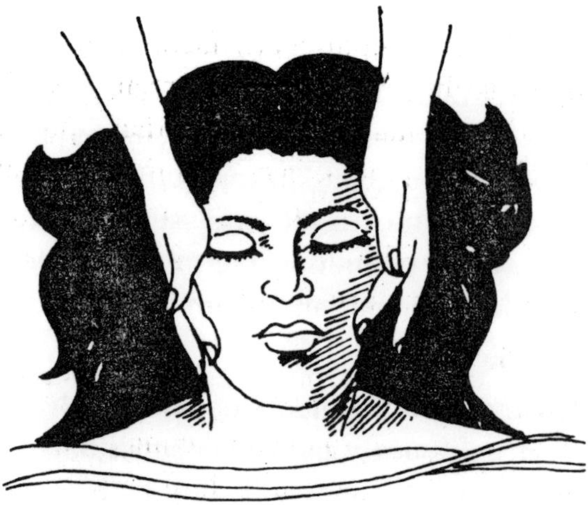

Massage of the face

CLEANSERS AND OILS

In this case only correct and suitable essential oils should be choosen that suit best your skin type. Blend suitables oils with unperfumed blend of some cleanser, tissue, off cream or lotion or liquid soap-these blended oils will discharge nature's duty in rebalancing your skin.

TONERS

The gentlest way to rejuvenate and tone up the skin is to use rose oil for dry, sensitive or normal skin and which hazel for oily skins—all these can be applied with cotton wool or sprayed on to the face for a more refreshing tone. For oral use, you can use herbal tea in fusions of neetle, rosehip, chamomile and marigold teas. If fresh herbs cannot be had, herbal tea bags may be used instead, dropping 2 drops of lavender or orange oil and let the same cool. For dry skins sandalwood or rose oils would suit better but for oily skins lemon grass and Juniper are preferred.

FACIAL OILS

Soft, supple, well-moisturised skin is reflective of healthy glow and also does not age so quickly. Hence use the most suitable facial oil. Most moisturisers sooth and sit on the skin surface while essential oils act from surface to dermis due to their five molecular structure. If the essential oil is in requisite proportion to a basic oil, they do not block skin pores on lubrication as they are so light that the skin can immediately absorb them. Add 6 drops of an essential oil to 6 tsp of base oil, keeping in mind an individual's requirements and sensitivity factor but not more than 3 variable oils should be blended with the base oil.

FACE MASKS

Face Masks can be processed from oatmeal and clay, pulverise fuller's earth that can be mixed into a paste with hot water—let it cool and then add yoghurt to make a smoother consistency. Similarly oatmeal can be reduced a fine powdered form and, then mixed into a paste. Thereafter, add 15 drops of the most suitable essential oil to a cupful of paste and let it cool, thereafter the same paste should be sponged off. For sensitive/dry skins add 3 tsp. of evening primrose to the base oil. Avoid contact with eyes while applying the face mask.

Caution : Sensitivity factor may undergo some change. Hence if an oil is suitable once it should not be taken for granted that the same will suit a person always—such a situation is more common in highly sensitive skins.

❑❑

8

SKIN CARE FOR ALL WEATHER

Along with stress and diet, environmental factors are one of the major causes of premature aging. Seasonal and climatic changes not only imbalance the subtle internal energies of the

body and mind, but also have an effect externally on the skin. Sun, wind and cold can be particularly damaging unless you take action to counter their effects.

SUN AND SKIN

The sun has always been a prime offender against the skin, but in recent years its harmful effects have increased as the protective ozone layer has weakened. Solar radiation is a factor in cataracts, cell degeneration and the breakdown of collagen and elastin, which leads to premature aging and wrinkles. It is the leading cause of skin cancer and also increases free radical generation in the skin because it decreases production of antioxidant enzymes. Drugs, such as blood pressure pills, diuretics and thorazine and foods and herbs such as artificial sweeteners, carbonated drinks, lemon, lime, carrot, fennel, parsley and bergamot are photosynthesisers. When ingested and absorbed into the body will cause hyperpigmentation, if the skin is exposed to too much sun. Of course, summer heat aggravates Bile in general, leading to increased skin sensitivity and increased sebaceous secretions.

In general, sensitive skin types tend to turn red rather than tan in the sun and also develop freckles. Dry and oily skin types both tan easily. Neverthless, nothing ages the skin more quickly than a sunburn, so individuals of every skin type should take precautions to protect themselves from the sun.

HOT WEATHER TIPS FOR BEAUTIFUL SKIN

❑ Warm weather is Bile season, so adjust your lifestyle and diet to avoid 'overheating'. Chlorinated pools, saltwater and sun dehydrate and age the skin, so the body needs extra moisture inside and out all summer long.

❑ Avoid sunbathing. If you want to be in the sun, stay active (do errands, take a walk), but it is better to stay out of the direct

Sun Bath

sun as much as possible. However, if you do sunbathe, olive and coconut oils are natural tanning agents, since they absorb ultraviolet light and provide even colouring. A daily dose of B-complex vitamins also helps produce an even tan.

❑ Use a sunscreen with an SPF of 15 to 30 depending upon your skin. If you don't burn easily but do tan easily, use lower SPF. If you burn more easily than you tan, use higher SPF. *Try not to use sunscreen unless you are in the sun,* since it tends to increase skin sensitivity in general.

❑ Sesame or neem oil both are excellent natural sunscreens according to Ayurveda.

❑ After sunbathing; take a cool bath, adding a few drops rose, sandalwood or vetiver essence to the water. Afterwards, pat the skin dry and when it is still moist, massage all over with your body oil.

❑ To treat sunburned skin, rub on either crushed cucumber, cucumber juice, aloevera juice, an ice infusion of elderflower and chamomile, or cold buttermilk.

WIND AND SKIN

Over exposure to dry, cold wind also damages the skin. In addition to their dehydrating effects, cold and wind put pressure on the epidermis, the horny protective top layer of skin which is composed of dead cells. When the cold and pressure are extreme, the dead cells desquamate—they burst—leaving the living, young cells of the derm layer exposed prematurely to the elements. As a result, the unprotected cells become inflamed, causing a characteristic tingling sensation on the skin, a problem that is particularly common among the elderly in the cold season. Too much peeling with acids produces the same result. The best protection against this effect is not face creams, but essential oils.

COLD WEATHER TIPS FOR BEAUTIFUL SKIN

❑ Cold weather and cool winds aggravate Air and cause dry skin conditions; so adjust your lifestyle and diet to add warmth, lubrication and moisture.

❑ Take fewer baths and showers in the cold season to avoid

dryness. When you do bathe, add a few drops of essential oil to the water to provide lubrication. Massage with oil before and after showering or bathing.

❑ Keep the temperature of your home as low as you comfortably can and use a humidifier or keep a bowl of water on your radiators to add moisture to the air.

❑ Take an occasional steam bath, but avoid saunas, which are dehydrating. Use petroleum jelly, if dryness persists.

❑ ❑

9

CARE FOR HEALTHY HAIR

Hair is mirror to one's health, whether it is a male or a female; apart from adding to one's personality. But health of hair can be adversely impacted due to mental, emotional and physical

Hair care is as important as you care for your body

disorders, or due to unbalanced diet, pollution factors etc. Moreover, to ensure healthy hair surface should also be massaged.

OILS FOR SCALP MASSAGE

Avoid using hair dyes, soaps, colourants acid. Instead use conditioners and shampoos that contain jojoba and almond oils. It is said that hot oil treatments permit (essential) oils to soak in easily and also condition the hair. Massage the scalp with warm oil, then wrap the head in a warm towel and, then leave it in the same position for half an hour or so.

Oils for Greasy Hair : Basil, Cedarwood, Chamomile, Cypress, Eucalyptus, Lemon Grass, Rosemary and Sage.

Oils for Normal Hair : Geranium, Lavender, Lemongrass, Rosemary.

Oils for Dry hair : Geranium, Lavender, Rose, Sandalwood, Ylang-Ylang.

METHOD TO MIX ESSENTIAL OILS WITH BASE OILS

You can use any base oil, that suits you the best, out of apricot kernel, sweet almond oil. Evening Primrose, Avocado, Jojoba or Sunflower. For massage on one scalp, you can choose upto 3 oils and use 5 drops of each oil to 30 ml base oil. For extra lengthier hair more quantity would be required. Put the bowl, containing blended oil in boiling hot water and then massage into the scalp, whereafter wrap the head with a hot towel and leave it off about 15 minutes and then shampoo.

GENERAL HAIR PROBLEMS

Mot of the hair related disorders are dependent on genetic, nutritional environmental and psychic conditions. When such conditions are massaged, the problem itself will get dispelled and such cases, no medical aid is called for. General hair care can be attended and maintained by proper hygienic and health rules.

HAIR LOSS

Do not be anxious if hair fall during and after combing. This condition surfaces consequent upon anxiety, stress and hormonal imbalance. So, learn how to relax and avoid tension. Seek guidance and advice of a Tricologist if there is some unusual thinning patch. But you can use blended oil of rosemary and lavender in a base oil for this condition.

DANDRUFF

Causes of dandruff are many and some of which are poor hair care, bad eating habits, unhealthy life style, chemical body changes, stress and wrong application of hair products. It is said that hot water baths also precipetate this condition, hence bath with lukewarm water, if weather conditions permit. For rinsing the hair use dandruff shampoos and conditioning rinses which are especially prepared for removal of dandruff. But blended essential oil also serves the purpose. Use cedarwood and lavender oil in a base oil for dry and itchy scalp, and for general treatment use oils of Tea Tree and patchouli. Massage into the scalp with these oils.

GREY HAIR

Long standing disease, worry, anxiety, stress, use of hair-dyes for colouring hair, poor diet and irregular eating habits, genetic factors etc. may cause hair to grey. First remove the contributory factor. Use essential oil enhance (like chamomile) to lighten hair and safe for darkening and discolourations.

SCALP MASSAGE

Massage of the scalp is an excellent way to stimulate the scalp, relieve tension and condition hair. If you have small hair, you can massage your scalp yourself but, for long hair, ask another

Scalp Massage

person to do the job for you. Following methods are advised, duly supported by illustrations, for massaging your scalp.

- Shampoo the hair and towel dry to absord excess water, comb through with a wide tooth comb. Tilt your head and pour some oil in the hairline. Massaging with thumbs on the temple and spread the fingers apart over the centre of head.

❑ Loosely run fingers and oil over the top of the top of the scalp from front to back lifting hair at the crown. Keep dipping your fingertips in the treatment oil to spread through the hair while massaging.

❑ Massage the head by kneading. Grip and push with finger pads rather than finger nails) against the scalp. The scalp should gently rotate against the skull. Concentrate on one area at a time with the hands positioned on either side of the scalp.

❑ Scalp massage works from front to back, from the forehead, frontal hairline, temples and sides, over the crown of the head to the base of the neck, following the natural flow of blood. If the scalp feel particularly tight then concentrate on areas where the scalp does not want to move. At the base of the skull, press firmly and push the whole scalp up towards the crown to release tension.

❑ Pull any extra hair oil through the hair, working out from the roots to the tips. Make sure all the hair is well coiled, and leave towel wrapped for at least 15 minutes before shampooing.

Note : Keep in mind the condition of your hair, use the most suitable oils (suggested earlier) for better results.

❑ ❑

10

ESSENTIAL OILS FOR SPECIFIC PROBLEMS AND AROMATIC BATH

Bathing, no doubt, is not merely a ritual but it has multiple benefits also, as water has remedial and relaxing properties. When bathing is preceded by an essential oil massage, it has multifold salutary effects. In Hindu religion, bathing is a way to healthy and hygenic life. Even in Greek and Roman cultures bathing was accorded a significantly important place. Bathing with essential oils can calm the agitated nerves, stimulate blood circulation, relax and deodorise the foul smelling body, uplift mood and remove the harmful foreign matters that cling to the body. There is a large list of essential oils out of which you can choose the most suitable oil(s) depending on your individual requirement and state of health.

Needless to remind that aromatic baths can help a lot in mitigating or even removing, the conditions like stiffness of joints, pains and aches, fatigues, colds, headaches, tone and condition the skin, relieve tension and anxiety and detoxify the body, remove foul odour and perspiration etc.

ESSENTIAL OILS FOR SPECIFIC PROBLEMS OF HEALTH

Oils for Relaxation : Basil, Bergamot, Cedarwood, Chamomile, Frankincense, Hyssop, Juniper, Lavender, Marjoram,

Melissa, Neroli, Patchouli, Rose, Sage, Sandalwood, Ylang-Ylang.

Oils for Stimulation : Cypress, Eucalpytus, Fennel, Geranium, Juniper, Lavender, Lemon, Lemon grass, Peppermint, Pine, Rosemary, Thyme.

Oils for Rheumatism/Arthritis : Chamomile, Eucalpytus, Juniper, Lavender, Rosemary, Thyme.

Oils for Eczema : Chamomile, Geranium, Hyssop, Juniper, Myrrh, Rosemary.

Oils for Dermatitis : Chamomile, Hyssop, Lavender.

Oils for Psoriasis : Bergamot, Chamomile, Lavender

If you study the above list, you can easily make out that oils like, Chamomile, Juniper, Rosemary, Lavender have been repeated quite often which implies that related disorders can be treated by using a specific oil for various applications and uses.

USE OF OILS FOR BATH

Essential oils make a bath both aromaticaly and therapeutically. They sink into the skin quickly and thoroughly apart from giving floral and herbal fragrances. If oil is added directly to the bath, it will float on the surface of bathing water, thus imparting the full aromatic benefits to you. To yield better and quicker results you can mix oil(s) in a base oil (like apricot kernel, sweet almond oil, Evening primrose or Jojoba base oils) and then, disperse the blended oil through the water.

While choosing oils make sure that they do not counter balance one another, rather they should complement and enhance the effect of other oils. Do not blend more than three essential oils at a time. Mix 5 drops of each type of oil to a 15 ml. of skin-softening oil (Stated earlier) base oil.

TEMPERATURE OF A RUNNING BATH

Time and temperature are important in a bath. Highly hot water is harmful and damaging in some diseases even though it increases heart beat and allows the capillaries and blood vessels to expand. Pregnant ladies, persons having high blood pressure, dandruff, piles, vericose veins must avoid hot water due to the above given reasons. Spend around 15-20 minutes in bath. Add diluted oils to water when the bath tub/buckets is full, and berver earlier, as these oils evaporate quickly.

RELAXATION BATH

Mark Evans suggests—"To calm yourself after a fraughtful day or to prepare yourself for a peaceful night's sleep, turn your bathroom into a private sanctuary. Keep the light soft, if possible, or use an eye-mask or burn aromatic candles. Support your head with a bath pillow, close your eyes and inhale deeply. Concentrate on your breathing, empty your mind and let the oil soothe away your stresses and strains. After a 15-20 minutes soak, get out slowly and wrap yourself in a large warm towel."

STIMULATING BATH

In this context Mark Evans adds—"Stimulating Bath is the best for the morning to get your start or to revive you before an evening out. Keep the water fairly cool and use an invigorating bath with to rub down and stimulate the circulation. When you have soaked, rinse yourself with water as cold as you can bear, either by splashing directly from the lap or shower, or by adding more cold water to cool down your bath. As you get out, either slap yourself dry to make the skin tingle or rub yourself vigorously with a towel.

SHOWERS AND COLD RINSES

Invigorating jets of water are ideal for getting the blood pumping and there is no need to forgo the benefits of aromatic oils. Skin tends to be sluggish in the cold winter months but sloughing off dead top layers can help regenerate cells and allow moisturizers to be absorbed more easily. An aromatic shower is an excellent way of aiding recovery from a certain illness, lifting the spirits, or promoting relaxation after a busy day. Showers and ideal for smoothing skin with exfoliating rubs using wet salt, a loofah or a mitt to slough off the top surface of dead skin cells. A dry friction glove or loofah is too harsh for

most skins so soften first in warm water. Soft bristle brushes can also help to get the circulation going with gentle massage on problem areas like hips or thighs. To keep friction brushes and mitts fresh always rinse them well and hang up to dry.

Essential oils can be used under the shower; try a base oil mixed with invigorating essences and with a clean face-cloth or sponge, pour on the oils and rub all over the body in circular motions whilst showering. To clear the sinuses and coughs and colds, sponge the chest with a mix of eucalyptus and peppermint oils. A cold water shower after cleansing improves the circulation and tightens skin pores.

Start off your shower or bath routine by whisking off dead skin cells with a friction mitt. Moisten the palm of the mitt with warm water or softening oils such as sweet almond or evening primrose. Concentrate on outer thighs, working from the knee in upward circular movements across the buttocks.

THE SENSUAL MASSAGE

"The power of perfume to inspire romance has been known since the Babyloninas, and perfume and flowers are still the favourable gifts for the lovers" and "The sense of smell is fundamental to our sensuality. Pheromones, chemicals secreted in human sweat, act as the most basic trigger to sexual attraction. The smells of flowers and plants are the plant equivalent of pheromones, irresistible to birds and bees and just as attractive to humans. We can use natural aromtic plant oils to relax, heighten our awareness, excite the senses and create a mood for love."

(Quoted from *'The Guide to Natural Living'*)

Sex desire and urge are the basic traits of humans and animals, though ways to express love and preactise romance, as a prelude to physical mating, may be (or generally are at variance. The author of *The Guide to Natural Living* has beautifully, succinctly and aesthetically explained use of various essential for setting the scene or say preparing and intitial atmosphere and a launching pad, preparing the body for romance and sexual cohabitation, massaging the partner and using oils to seducting the partner.

PREPARING YOURSELF AND THE PARTNER FOR ROMANCE

Romance is always a bilateral experience. If you ignore your partner and look towards your own interest(s), you will not be able to enjoy neither romance nor sex. So it is necessary to create sensual and calming atmosphere. To begin with, light some scented candles or evaporate a few drops of pleasing essential oil in light bulb ring or a fragrance whereafter dim the light and turn up the heat. You can also sprinkle a few drops of Jasmine or Rose oils on your pillows or drop 3 drops of your favourite oil to your bedsheet or drop 3 drops in bath water before you actually rinse or keep aromatic bags/scented balls in the drawers. Even flowers of Jasmine and Rose, if scattered on your bed, will ignite libido and also create sensual atmosphere in the room.

Remember it is always necessary to dispsel any foul odour from the body, mouth, nose and armpits and, if you take an aromatic bath, you can easily rid your body of all such nauseating smells. Next comes aromatic baths where both the partners should participate and rinse each other's body with scented oils. After taking bath you should also dab your temples, wrists, armpits, area behind the ears and knees and allow enough time to your partner to explore your body as a whole and, more particularly the erogenous zones.

SENSUAL MASSAGE BY THE PARTNER

Ladies take longer time in sexual arousal, hence the male partner should preferably massage his female partner. It would be still better if both equally participate in body massage and enjoy the gradual experience of touch and smell. It also helps to soothe mental agitation, relaxes body and mind, is a prelude to more joyous sexual union. It is an excellent total physical experience that stimulates sensuality. In order to excite surface of the skin, you can kneading with your fingertips to excite the surface. Use plenty of effluerage all over the body to excite tense areas of the body. For both the purposes use some basic essential oils. But do not resort to any lymph drainage movements as they prove counter-productive and are also unerotic. Do not do any act that turns

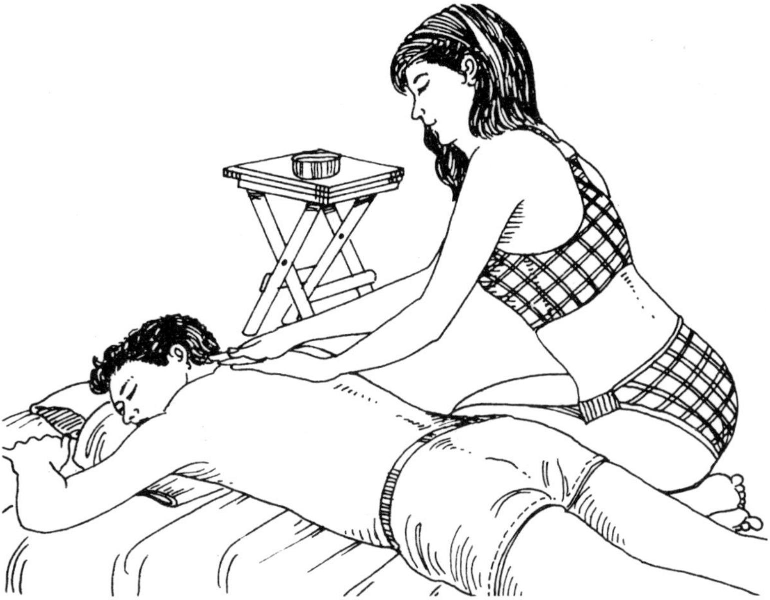

Jasmine and Rose oil ignite passions and create sexual atmosphere

your partner off and keep a track of her preferences and sensitivity. Explore your partner's inside of thighs and underarm areas, explore her feet and ears, massage her pubic areas. Let her feel comfortable and enjoy each and every stroke, touch and sense of smell. Be patient and do not hasten—at least wait till she herself beseeches you to have sex. During sensual body massage keep your passions under control and avoid a 'quickie'.

PROPERTIES OF ESSENTIAL OILS FOR SEDUCTION

Do not blend too many oils at a time as they may clash with each other or even create a sense of "Turn off". All aphrodiasic essential oils do not suit all individuals alike, hence work out your preference, keeping in mind your partner's preferred choices also. You can select an oil or oils of your choice keeping view the undernoted properties of the oils.

- **Jasmine :** Floral fragnance of this oil creates a pleasing luxurious atmosphere and boosts up confidence.
- **Rose :** It is an extremely powerful oil for seduction, but is perhaps the costliest of all the oils.

- **Sandalwood :** It is a woody oil, exotic and sweet with icy undertones.
- **Ylang-Ylang :** It gives a feeling of utmost relaxation, its floral scent has long lasting effect. It also gives a feeling well-being. It is also useful in the case of frigidity and impotency.
- **Geranium :** Because of its strong floral scent, it uplifts moods and relaxes also.
- **Neroli :** It helps to win over inhibitions and shyness due to its sweet and freshening fragrance.
- **Patchouli :** It heightens the senses, is stimulating even in small doses, is heavy and exotic.
- **Clarysage :** It is sensuous, slightly intoxicating and sweet. But if used in high doses, its sedative effect will inhibit sex drive and urge. Hence use only in moderate and lower doses.

In addition to the above mentioned oils, you may also try cardamom, cinnamon, ginger, or black pepper as they have spicy, exotic and warm properties. Due to their capacity to overpower easily, use them rather sparingly.

Finally, it is advised that momentum of seduction and romance is built up gradually and not in a hush. If you are awfully hasty, you will end up as a dismal failure, much to the chagrin of your partner and yourself. First try to soothe your mental agitation, physical fatigue or any type of tension. Feel relaxed and cheerful.

❑ ❑

11

CARE OF BODY PARTS

Essential oils impart pleasure and health benefits, as they absorb quiteably into the warm and damp skin. To prepare body oil choose three bath essential oils (5 drops of each oil) in 2 tbsp (or 30 ml) base oil. In case you wish to prepare larger quantity of body oil, you can use a 3% concentration of essential oil to the base oil. Now, after you have prepared a suitable body oil, you can proceed give an after-bath treatment to your body, as suggested hereunder.

HANDS AND NAILS

Hands and nails get affected after daily routine work and if hands are dirty, the dirt will pass on to our stomach with the eaten food. If the filth gets stuck within the nails, it can cause multiple infections. Hence care and hygiene of both hands and nails is pre

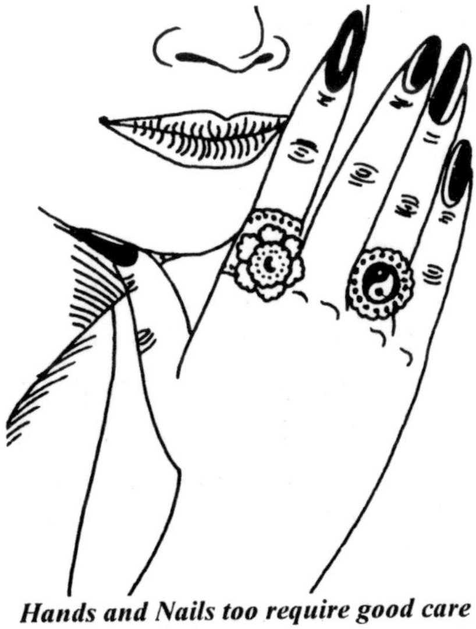

Hands and Nails too require good care

requisite for our health. If hands are dipped or soaked in water during a bath, the skin gets tender and softer—it will help to clean around the nails and also clip even uneven nails without snagging. Hence the most ideal time for pedicure or manicure is after soaking the hands. For flanky and fragile nails need nourishing and rich treatment, for which they should be rubbed with oil of apricot kernel, jojoba oil or wheatgerm oil. For moisturising and soothing the hands mix 5 drops each of lavender, lemon and patchouli oils to 15 ml of sweet almond oil and apply over hands.

CONDITIONING OF HANDS AND NAILS

Hand and nails should be conditioned by way of a simple finger-pulling exercise.

Stretch and spread the fingers straight out. Now massage each finger with blending oils—starting from the tip of the nails to the cuticles and upto the knuckle of each finger.

ELBOWS

Elbows are generally neglected during and after bath. But such a neglect can result in build up of hard protective layers of grey and unsightly skin. Certain persons have tougher and rough skin around the elbow. But the problem can be easily encountered by application of sweet almond oil and fine oatmeal, for which 3 tbsp each of sweet almond oil and fine oatmeal should be mixed to prepare a paste, add yoghurt or milk to it. This paste should be rubbed over the elbows and any grey spot and goosey areas of skin around the upper arms. If arms are flabby add to the past 6 drops of fennel oil also.

Another cheaper and traditional method to cut a lemon into 2 pieces, squeeze out the juice and then rub the elbow in the hollow of the lemon. Some persons mix lemon juice and glycerine also for the same purpose, adding also a few drops of sweet oil of almond. Oil is being applied to the arms with smooth upward strokes. You should concentrate more on the elbows and upper arms where the skin is often found to be drier and rougher.

FEET

Feet are the most neglected part of our body as we take care of them when they are hurt, or pain or ache. Remember, feet have to carry the burden of the entire body and, if feet are tired, aching or hurt, our mobility will be restricted. Moreover, at feet lower extremities also end. While treating your feet, take particular care

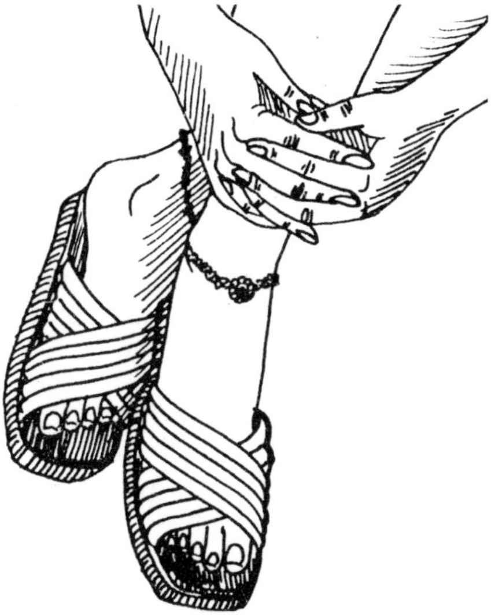

Oil massage gives relief to the tired feet

of beds, soles and toes. Whenever you feel your feet are fatigued or start aching, it is nature's warning signal. While treating your feet after a bath, treat both the feet in entirely and do not adopt a lopsided and casual approach. As skin on and around heels is quite hard, it should be polished hard (around heels and soles) with the help of a punice stone or damp salt. If you want to stimulate blood circulation and also relax your tired feet, you should bend one knee (while in the bath) grip the toes first and thereafter massage in an upward direction—starting from the toes and then going upwards to heels and finally to calves. Body oil should be massaged into the feet after you have taken a bath or shower or pedicure.

Add 3 drops each of lavender and cypress oils to a basin full of water (so as to gain deidrising and soothing effect) and bathe your feet. If you have chiblains, mix 3 drops of geranium and one drop each of rosemary and lavender oils to 1 tbsp of base oil of sweet almond and then massage the affected parts.

Massage in between the toes (after a bath) and then move around the tougher skin and heel areas, in order to soften the feet. In order to stimulate blood circulation to each hook and corner of the feet, finish with sweeping movements all over the area.

APPLYING BODY OIL TO NECK, SHOULDERS AND BACK

As it is quite difficult to reach the areas of neck, shoulders and back either, during or after a bath, these remain neglected, even though these area and skin around them should be nourished to release tension. Massage the said areas with a suitable body oil as smoothly as possible. It is better to seek another person's help in this regard.

❑❑

12

MASSAGE OF LEGS AND HAND

This process consists of two methods, *viz* effleurage and leg stretching. The term 'effleurage' means that when a masseur passes his/her hands continuously and rhythemically over a person's skin in one direction only, with the aim of increasing the flow of blood in that direction and aiding the dispersal of any swelling due to oedema.)

EFFLEURAGE

To begin with apply oil to both the legs using effleurage movement working from the ankles upwards, as in the same manner as detailed in the case of massage back of the legs. In order to ensure even distribution of oil, repeat the sequence of effleurage several times.

LEG STRETCH

Support the leg at the ankle and behind the knee, bend the leg up and place the same in line with the shoulder. Clasp your hands

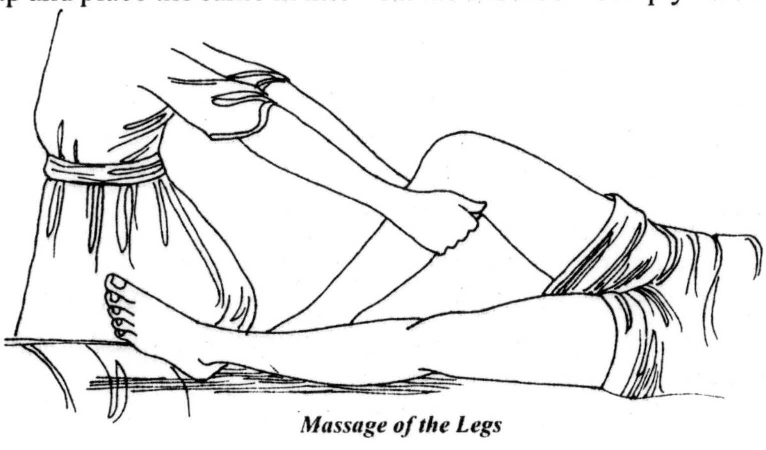

Massage of the Legs

around the back of the knee and ask your partner to inhale deeply, then pull the calf muscle toward you. Hold the calf muscle for a slow count of 3. When your partner breathes out, release your pull on the calf muscles.

Above detailed movement should be repeated 3 times, after which let the leg be laid down. Then, repeat the stretch on the other leg also.

EFFLEURAGE ON HANDS AND ARMS

- Be seated to the side of your partner and, then slightly move one arm away from her. Now apply oil from just above the wrist, upto the shoulder and round.
- Now your first arm should come off the arm, while the other hand will start (movement) at the wrist and sweep uptoward the gland that is seated in the joint of elbow.

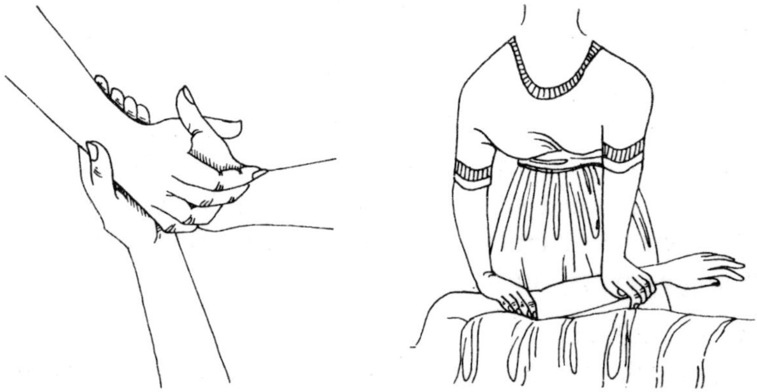

Massage of the Hands and Arm

- Now the first hand should cross the second hand as it reaches the elbow and sweeps again from wrist to the shoulder.

Repeat this movement 6-7 times on one leg and, then, repeat the same process on the other leg also.

HAND MASSAGE

When you have finished the above described movements on both the legs, you can follow the effleurage with flushing to the inside of the arm, using the same movements performed on the leg, working from the wrist to the elbow. Before going on to the second arm, massage the hand of the first are.

Hand Massage

- ❑ Rest your partner's palm of hand over your palm, and use small brushing movements with the help of your thumbs so as to work upward between the joints of the fingers towards the wrist.
- ❑ Pulling back to the fingers, gently massage the joint between your thumb and forefinger as you draw towards the tips of fingers. Then finish up with a slight pull to the finger so as to stretch it out.
- ❑ Repeat the process with finger, finally finishing with the thumb.

Repeat the identical movements on the other hand and arm also.

When you have finished the massage the partner should be covered upto the knee and make sure that she is completely relaxed, comfortable and warm. Now let her relax or rest for 5-15 minutes. After requisite rest, help your partner in sitting up rather carefully and after a glassful of water is required.

❑ ❑

BABY MASSAGE

Massage is a marvellous way to enhance the natural bounding between the mother and the (new born) baby as touch is a natural way to establish contact between both. All babies instantly respond to cuddling and caressing. You must have noticed how a baby

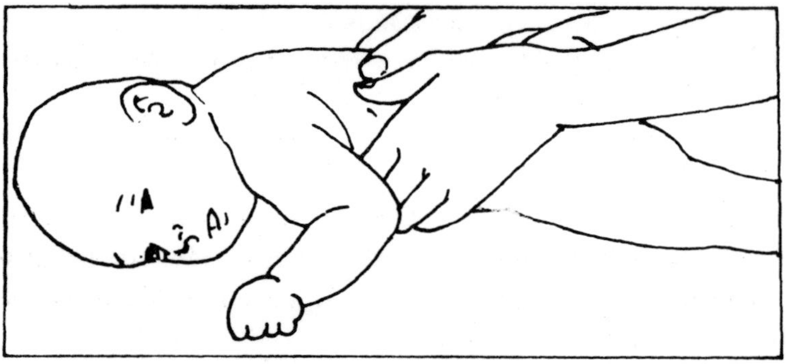

Back massage of the Baby

tightly curls its hands and feet when touched. Since I have given reasonably detailed account of massage with blending of essential oils with carrier oils in the case of elders but in the case of babies, no essential oil is used, but only light vegetable oils, like sweet almond, sunflower and baby oil or olive oil are used.

ADVANTAGES AND SIGNIFICANT POINTS

- Unless okayed by an aroma therapist, no essential oil should be added to the massage oil.
- Do not expose baby's tender skin to strong or biting cold, cold winds and snow fall.
- Warm your hands before the massage. It is still better if oil is also slightly warmed.

- ❑ Gently stroke baby's tender body and do not exert any pressure.
- ❑ Do not massage when the baby is weeping or is ill or when he resists any type of touch even.
- ❑ Room should be warm, quiet and without any draughts.
- ❑ Massage relieves babies colic, alleviates wind, improves digestion, cures coughs, and colds etc.
- ❑ Keep movements gentle and smooth flowing.
- ❑ Massage builds up general resistance of body.
- ❑ Do not apply any oil to baby's face and eyes.
- ❑ Do not massage immediately before, during or after a feed.

Make sure that massage helps your baby to feel lighter and better and that no discomfort or agitation is caused to it. If the baby weeps or cries during the massage, it means the massage area is either painful or too sensitive. In such a situation stop massaging. You may restart when the baby feels comfortable.

PROCEED

Take a large sized towel and spread half portion there of on your legs or on laps and the other half uner the baby's back but ensure there are no wrinkles or folds. Lay the baby on its back, or lay him in the position that makes him feel comfortable. Apply some oil to your palms and, then, apply gently and softly over the frontal portion of his body. Use oil of sweet almond 5 ml. Ensure that your hands are warm, room is also warm and quiet, and also there are no draughts. You can massage baby's body either before the bath or after the bath, but ideal time should preferably is said to be after the time.

FRONTAL MASSAGE

❑ Gently and slowly apply a little quantity of the oil over its front of the body, from shoulders to feet, but avoid the face. Now lightly stroke down the chest and abdomen using the tips of your fingers. By your light and delightful strokes, you can calm your baby at any time. Remember, touch of hands to the body will cheer up the baby and he will show his happiness through light laughter or innocent smile. Let his legs be kept in a straight line but if he curls up his legs, let him do so. It is a sign that he is enjoying and releasing the movements.

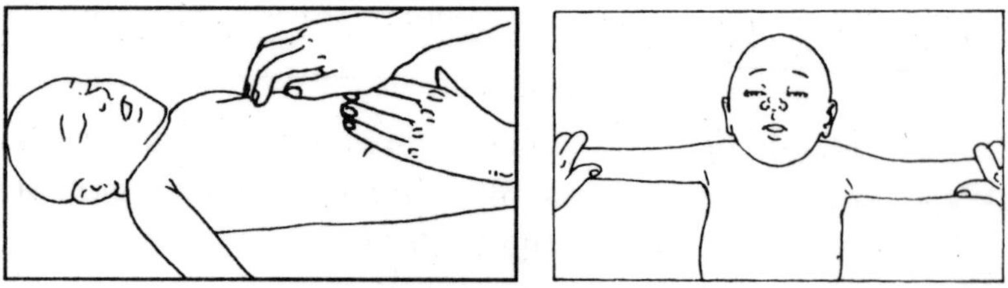

Frontal massage of the Baby

❑ Keep the pressure very light, move both your hands smoothly in continuous and circular strokes over the abdomen, working up the baby's right side across and down his body's left side. Keep your movements continuous by lifting your left hand when your arms cross. Now repeat such circular movements many a time.

LEFT SIDE MASSAGE

❑ If your baby lets you, gently stretch out both the arms to the sides, spreading hands and fingers. Then gently squeeze out along the arms and, with light and circular thumb movements massage his palms and wrists. Before you finish your movements, do not forget to stretch out his each finger with a light pull.

❑ Now move on to legs and feet, but work out only on one leg at a time. Supporting baby's leg with both of your hands gently squeeze and release fleshy part of his thigh. Thereafter, support the leg with one hand and stroke the leg, from knee to the thigh and back down again.

RIGHT SIDE MASSAGE

Now move your supporting hand down to behind the ankle. Then gently smooth palm of your hand over top of baby's foot—that is from toe to ankle and back again. As you reach the toes, stretch each toe very gently, without exerting any force/pressure.

The same steps should be repeated 4-5 times on baby's other leg also.

BACK SIDE MASSAGE

❑ Now turn the baby over onto the front. Then start to stroke up his entire back side so that applied oil is evenly distributed to the whole of the back side. After applying the oil evenly over his back side, work up your strokes around baby's side also, and then

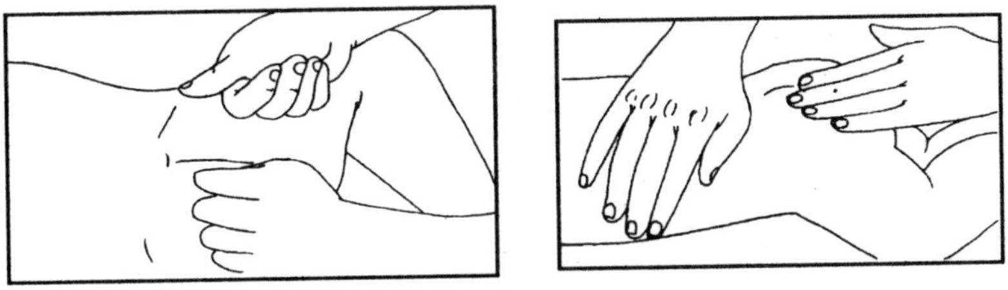

Back side massage

up the legs, back and out over the arms. If you massage his back side, as suggested, it will have very calming impact on the baby's spinal nerves, because soothing effect always cheers the baby up.

❑ To stimulate the blood circulation, gently knead and sqeeze its buttocks. For this you should make a loose fist and rotate over the baby's buttocks in circular movements.

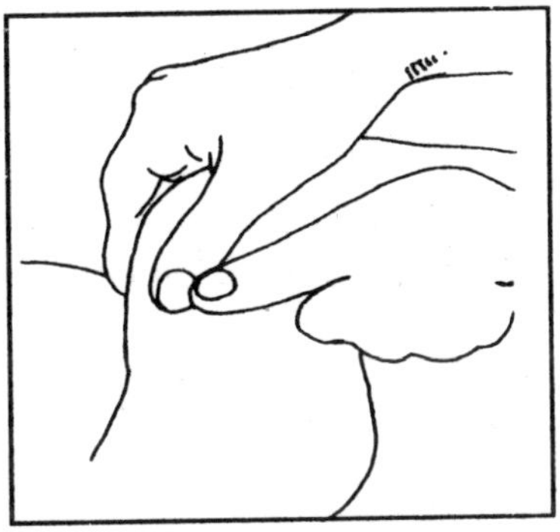

❑ Now gently stroke up one side of the back to the shoulders and down again. Repeat the suggested movements on the other side of the back also.

❑ Now bring both of your hand's around the scetes of your body and, then, using your thumbs, massage gently up the back to the base of the neck. You should also massage baby's shoulders with the help of thumbs.

❑ Finally, before you finish up, repeat the feather strokes that were used at the beginning of the massage, by working all over the back, from neck to buttocks.

See, how a baby feels happy, cheerful and relaxed when its mother holds it in her hands, looks into its eyes, communicates with the baby in a motherly affectionate and

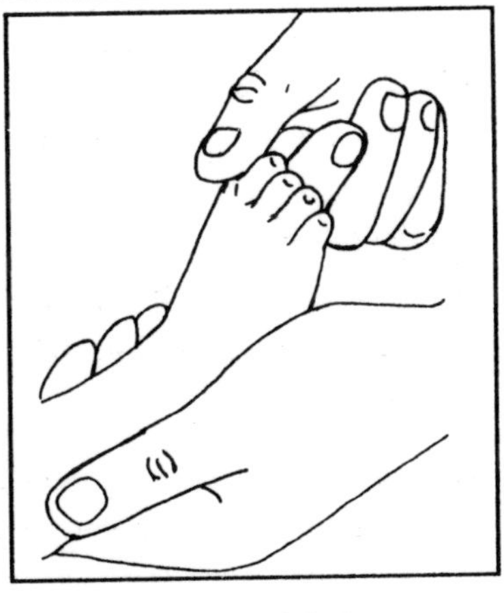

Massgage of the legs

caressing mood. There is also a sort of indirect exercise for the baby. It is simply a cheerful reaction of affirmity, affection, touch and nearness. When the infant laughs, its lungs expand, fresh air lets in, skin smoothen, eyes sparkle and body reverbrates with renewed energy. If you cling her to your breast, she will feel still reassured, secure and filled up with confidence.

MASSAGE FOR EVERYONE

Remember as a child if you bumped your head (or anywhere else) a wise adult would kindly rub it better? Or that if any part of your body aches now it's instinctive to put your hand there?

Very simply, this how massage works. Touch is both healing and comforting and, what's more, we can all enjoy the pleasures of it—both giving and receiving. massage is beneficial to us in several different ways and:

- ❑ Improves blood circulation
- ❑ Calms the nervous system
- ❑ Stimulates skin function
- ❑ Improves muscle tone
- ❑ Eases aches and pains in muscles and joints

And it feels marvellous!

❑❑

14

AROMATHERAPY AND PREGNANCY

The gentle, healing action of aromatherapy is particularly helpful during pregnancy, when it is not advisable to take medication except under the watchful eye of your doctor.

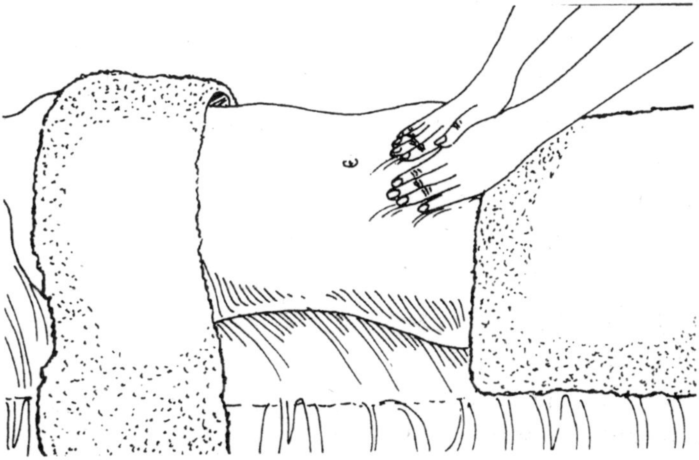

Aromatherapy is very useful during pregnancy

You will see how aromatherapy oils can help to lessen the niggly, uncomfortable problems, such as nausea (morning sickness), swollen hands and feets, general aches and pains and fatigue. They can also help you to relax, and look after your body as it slowly goes through changes. Please be sensible, though. If there's anything you're unsure of regarding your health, do check with your doctor first.

IN THE BEGINNING (FIRST TO THIRD MONTH)

The first three months of pregnancy are the most taxing for

your body. During these early stages 'blooming' may be the last thing you feel. Rest is very important, so allow time to relax and wind down before going off to bed. You could also try burning one of the relaxing base note oils in your bedroom, to help you sleep.

You may feel nauseous, particularly between the eighth and tenth weeks, when one of the pregnancy hormones is at its peak.

Your skin and hair can take a bashing early on in pregnancy when a sudden increase in your hormone levels activates the sebaceous glands, increasing the oiliness of your skin and hair. Luckily, this usually corrects itself during the next few months, but you should be extra scrupulous right now and, if necessary, reassess your skin type.

FATIGUE

Try to relax prior to going to bed. Either try a relaxing aromatherapy bath or burn one of the following blends of oil in the room you are in before going off to bed, then take the burner/ vaporizer into your bedroom.

- ❑ Camomile and lavender
- ❑ Sandalwood
- ❑ Neroli and ylang-ylang

THE MIDDLE MONTHS (FOURTH TO SIXTH MONTH)

Nausea, tiredness and irritability should all have lifted by now, and you will probably feel you can take on the world. This is a good time to start making your body more flexible, and to learn relaxation and breathing techniques. Aromatherapy oils are great aids to relaxation, so don't overlook them.

Start to look after your skin (on both your face and body) religiously now. It may seem a chore, but it will pay dividends later. Your weight will have increased quite noticeably already, putting extra strain on your pelvis, back and legs. Varicose veins and spider veins often first appear during pregnancy, so try to take as many preventive measures as possible now. Support tights help, as do regular moderate exercise and the aromatherapy treatment.

Constipation can sometimes be a problem in the early stages of pregnancy, but avoid the use of laxatives. Instead, try to eat high-fibre and raw foods and drink plenty of water, or try the aromatherapy remedy.

MORNING SICKNESS OR NAUSEA

If you're feeling nauseous, but not actually, vomiting, mix up a blend of two drops each of fennel, lavender and sandalwood oils with 4 fl oz (100 ml) of a carrier oil. Massage it into your abdomen at regular intervals during the day, and try a little dabbed under your nose so you can inhale it. Inhaling peppermint oil can also relieve morning sickness, but it would be advisable to massage with it during pregnancy.

VOMITING

If you're vomiting, mix up a blend of two drops each of lemon, fennel and rose oil with 4 oz (100 ml) of a carrier oil. Gently massage it into your upper and lower abdomen, and also inhale it-if you can bear it.

CONSTIPATION

Try to relieve your constipation naturally by watching your diet (eat more unrefined food) and increasing your liquid intake. A helpful aromatherapy mixture is three drops of black pepper and three drops of fennel oil in 4 fl oz (100 ml) of a carrier oil. Gently massage it along your lower abdomen, starting just inside your right hip bone, work up, then across past your navel and back down towards your left hip bone. Be gentle and repeat several times daily.

TIRED LEGS/VARICOSE VEINS

Add three drops of lemon and three drops of lavender oil 4 doz (100 ml) of a light carrier oil, such as grapeseed oil. Massage daily (twice a day, if time allows) from the ankle firmly up to the knee, then firmly up to the top of the thigh. Repeat these movements until the oil is absorbed. After the treatment try to spend at least half an hour with both feet raised above hip level.

Note : Try to avoid very hot baths as they can weaken the capillaries and cause little broken veins under your skin,

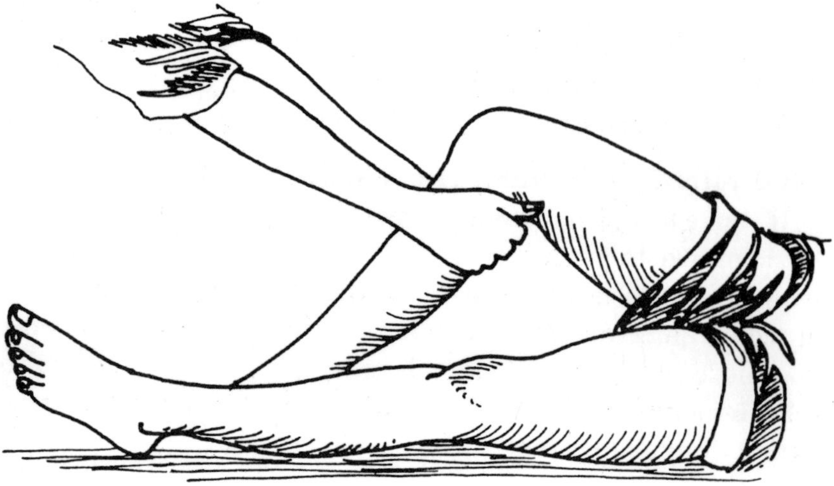

Massage for tired legs

particularly on your thighs. You are extra vulnerable to these during pregnancy.

THE FINAL MONTHS (SEVEN TO NINE MONTH)

By now you will be carrying an extra 15 pounds (6.75 kilos) or more in weight. You will probably tire quickly and may even sometimes feel dizzy. Sleep can become a problem as it is difficult to find a comfortable position in bed.

Try lying on your side with a cushion under your uppermost leg, knees slightly bent. The cushion acts as a support and will lessen the strain on your lower back.

Towards the end of pregnancy a lot of women find their hands and feet swell up, especially during hot weather. Counteract this by drinking plenty of water (to aid kidney function) and trying the appropriate aromatherapy treatment.

DIFFICULTY IN SLEEPING

Ask your partner to gently massage your lower back, shoulders and neck with an aromatherapy blend made from three drops of vetivert and three drops of lavender oil in 4 fl oz (100 ml) of a carrier oil. This is a sedative, being calming and relaxing, and it has certainly helped patients through some sleepless nights.

You can also try drinking camomile tea before going to bed, and put a little of the above blend on your pillow.

FLUID RETENTION

Mix two drops of eucalyptus oil, two drops of geranium oil and two drops of lavender oil with 4 fl oz (100 ml) of a light carrier oil. Rub it gently into your lower legs and hands. Massage with firm upward strokes - on your legs from ankle to knee, on your arms from hand to elbow. You can also try using the blend in a coolish bath.

SORE NIPPLES

Your breasts will have grown larger throughout pregnancy, and you may have noticed your nipples have darkened and become softer. From the middle months onwards drops of colostrum (the baby's first food if you breast feed) are secreted from your nipples and sometimes they can become sore and cracked.

The following aromatherapy treatment is healing and soothing, and can be continued while you breast feed. Add six drops of marigold oil (often known as calendula) to 4 fl oz (100 ml) of a carrier oil (wheatgerm oil is good). Apply two or three times a day. You can add the marigold oil to a fragrance-free cream, if you prefer.

GENTLE WAYS TO MASSAGE

I've already talked at length about the benefits of massage. It is an excellent way for you and your partner to get to know the feel

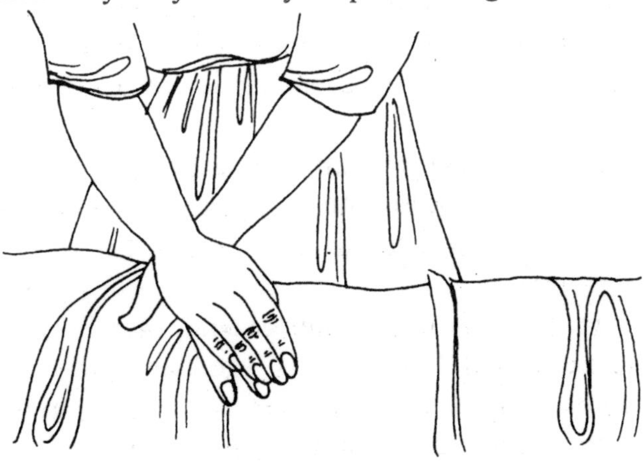

Utmost care and precaution should be taken during pregnancy

of your body, and the way it is changing, throughout pregnancy. Obviously, extra care needs to be taken when working on more vulnerable areas, such as your tummy and lower back, but they can still be worked on, and you will find here some nice, gentle massage movements to try.

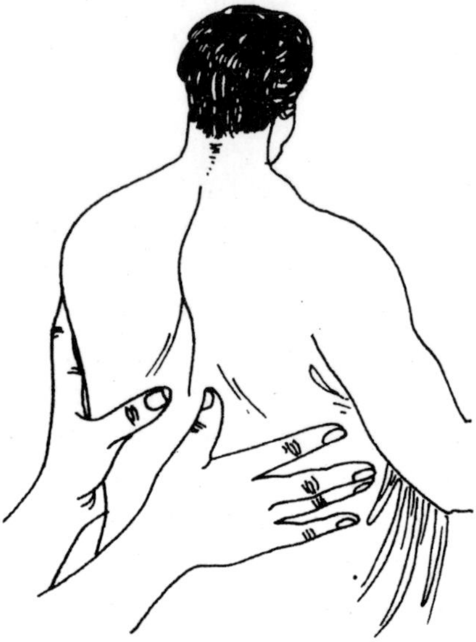

Massage of the back

During pregnancy, the amount of aromatherapy oil you add to the carrier oil should be reduced by half, because your body is much more sensitive to the oils when you are pregnant, and better able to absorb them. Nevertheless, you will still receive an effective treatment, so don't be tempted to add a few more drops just in case.

This relaxation massage is simple to learn, and you could even give it to a pregnant friend. The lovely aromatherapy scents are also relaxing and help alleviate tension which is often present during pregnancy.

Make sure your partner is comfortable, then begin. If your partner is more than four months' pregnant she will find it uncomfortable to lie on her front. Instead, help her to lie on her side supported by a cushion, or massage her back while she is in a sitting position, with a cushion to lean on for support.

MASSAGING THE BACK

Gently apply your chosen oil to your partner's back, shoulders and arms.

❑ Stroke gently down the spine from the base of the neck to the lower back. Do this slowly and evenly and repeat, using alternate hands, twenty times.

❑ With both hands, gently stroke down the sides of the neck, over the shoulders and down the arms, coming off at the hands. Repeat ten times.

❑ With both hands, stroke gently up the spine, round the shoulder blades in a figure-of-eight, then gently down the sides of the body. Repeat ten times.

❑ Stoke across the back, starting from the lower back on the right hand side. Stroke in from the outside of the body towards the spine with alternate hands, moving gently up the back towards the shoulders. Repeat several times on the right side, then work on the left side in the same way.

❑ Place one hand on your partner's lower back, place your other hand on top, and allow the heat from your hands to build up. This is very soothing to a sore back.

❑ Repeat step 1.

Now work on your partner's neck to ease tension.

❑ Knead along from the outer shoulders towards the base of the neck. Repeat four or five times.

❑ With your fingertips, work in little circular movements from the base of the neck up to the base of the skull. Repeat four or five times.

❑ Stroke down the sides of the neck and out to the shoulders, very slowly. Repeat five or six times.

Now turn your partner on to her back. (She may like the support of a rolled-up towel under her knees.)

MASSAGING THE TUMMY

Gently apply your chosen oil to your partner's tummy.

❑ Gently stroke down the tummy from between the breasts to the public bone. Repeat twenty times with alternate hands.

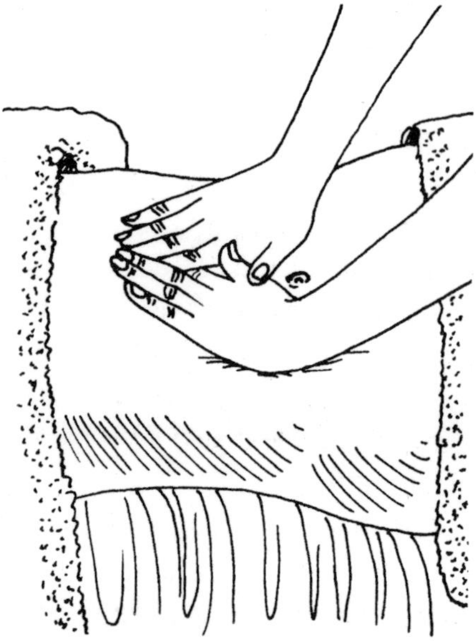

Massage of the stomach

❑ Gently circle around the tummy with the flat of your hand in a clockwise direction. Do not apply any pressure. Think of this as a way to soothe and calm your partner. Repeat five or six times.

❑ Stroke in from the hip bone, using alternate hands, gradually moving up the body to the side of the chest. Repeat several times on each side.

❑ The movement is helpful for an aching, tired back. Repeat under your partner's waist with both hands. Now slide them out from under her back, lifting gently as you do so. Bring your hands gently over her tummy. Repeat five or six times.

❑ Repeat step 1.

The massage is mainly for relaxation, and I would recommend that you try one of the following aromatherapy blends. Use six drops of aromatherapy oil to 4 fl oz (100 ml) of carrier oil.

❑ Camomile and lavender

❑ Frankincense and neroli

❑ Ylang-ylang and sandalwood

❑ Geranium and rose

Alternatively, use any of the above oils singly in a carrier oil.

❑ ❑

15

AROMATHERAPY DURING LABOUR

The experience of labour is different for every women, as I've found out through treating lots of women through their pregnancies and on after their baby has been born. What they do agree on, however, is the importance of being able to relax, and that the touch of their partner is both reassuring and relieving.

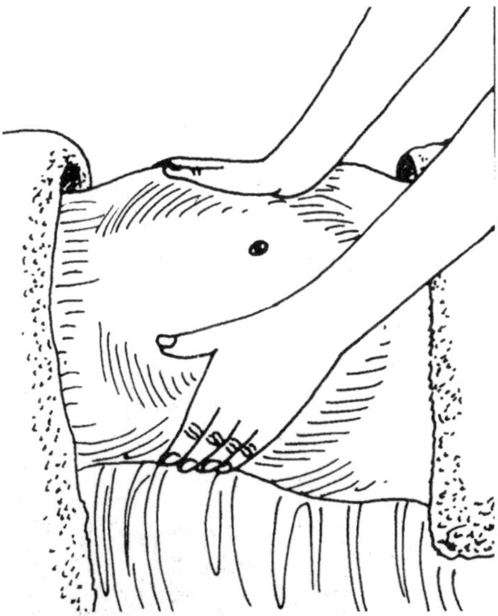

Aromatherapy during labour helps to relax

Using aromatherapy massage during labour helps you to relax and cope with the contractions, and it can also reduce the tension and fear you will naturally feel because of its calming effect on your nervous system. You may find that early on in labour you like the feeling of quite firm pressure but as your contraction become more intense gentle strokes may be all you can bear. It's up to you.

If you've already experienced aromatherapy massage earlier in your pregnancy your partner will have an idea of the kind of touch that is most helpful to you.

TUMMY MASSAGE

This is helpful in the earlier stages of labour, and the movements are soothing when the contractions feel like period pains. Use three drops of camomile or lavender oil in 4 fl oz (100 ml) of a light carrier oil.

❑ Using relaxed hands, make a fingure-of-eight movement across the tummy and under the 'bump'. This movement should be fairly light, especially if the tummy is tender.

❑ Gently stroke around the bump, using your fingertips in a circular movement.

Repeat these movements as necessary.

BACK SOOTHER

Again, use three drops of camomile or lavender oil in 4 fl oz (100 ml) of a carrier oil.

Back Soother

❑ With the heel of your hand apply pressure to the small of the back. Gently move your hand in an anti-clockwise circular movement while keeping firm contact with the skin.

❑ Place one hand on top of the other in the small of the back and allow heat to build up under your hands.

These movements are helpful for contractions felt in the lower back.

If you are feeling too sensitive to be massaged or even touched on your body, try the following aromatherapy relaxers.

FACE SOOTHER

Add a few drops of lavender or rose oil to some chilled rosewater. Dip a small face sponge into this mixture, then smooth it over your forehead, down your face and neck, gently and rhythmically. Alternatively, your partner can do this for you. The flowery aroma is very comforting, and helps to take your mind away from the labour pains.

SCENTED WATER SOOTHER

Kneeling in a deep, warm bath can be soothing in the earlier stages of labour, and the addition of relaxing aromatherapy oils intensifies this experience. Choose from:

❑ Camomile
❑ Ylang-ylang
❑ Lavender
❑ Geranium

Your partner can help take your mind off the pains by rhythmically pouring warm, scented water down your back.

HAND SOOTHER

When the contractions become difficult, this simple touch is very reassuring and helps to create a feeling of safety.

❑ Ask your partner to rub a little lavender oil (in a carrier oil) into the solar plexus on your hand.

❑ Now, he or she can gently stoke and soothe your hand, keeping a reassuring contact with you. Concentrate on relaxing into the touch.

ONE FOR YOUR PARTNER

If he or she is becoming weary, inhaling the following can help. Inhale neat:

- ❑ Rosemary
- ❑ Neroli
- ❑ Petigrain
- ❑ Lavender
- ❑ Peppermint

❑ ❑

16

HELP FOR STRETCH MARKS

Stretch marks are actually little tears in the tissue beneath the skin surface, and they show up first as red or purplish marks which fade to a silvery white scar. They are caused by the skin stretching as your weight increases, and you are more prone to them during

Breats too need proper care

pregnancy when your weight gain is rapid. Some skins have a better capacity to stretch than others, so pregnancy doesn't necessarily mean you'll get stretch marks. Although I don't believe that by applying oils and lotions you can prevent stretch marks (the damage occurs quite deep in the skin), you can help to keep your skin elastic and supple. Also, by using aromatherapy oils, you can minimize the scarring and speed up the skin's healing process.

AROMATHERAPY STRECH MARK OIL

Add three drops of frankincense and three drops of tangerine oil to a carrier blend of 2 fl oz (50 ml) of avocado oil and 2 fl oz (50 ml) of wheatgerm oil. Frankincense has a rejuvenating effect on your skin and tangerine oil is rich in Vitamin C and helps to maintain your skin's elasticity.

I recommend you start using this blend from the beginning of your pregnancy, paying special attention to your breasts, tummy, hips and thighs. Massage it gently into all those areas at least once a day. A good time to do this is at night, after your bath, when your skin is soft.

You may also like to try the following breast massage, as your breasts will increase in size during pregnancy and are therefore prone to stretch marks and tissue damage.

BREAST MASSAGE

Apply the stretch mark oil to your breasts.

❑ Gently work around each breast in a circular movement with your whole hand. Repeat five or six times.

Breast Massage

❑ Now, place the heel of each hand on either side of one breast and gently stroke in towards the nipple. Repeat five or six times.

❑ Next, move your hands to the top and underside of the breast and again stroke into the nipple. Repeat five or six times.

❑ Gently stretch each nipple with your fingertips.

❑ Repeat step 1.

❑ ❑

17

SIMPLE BODY MASSAGE

Just before you begin your massage check that your hands and clean and your nails fairly short with no jagged edges. Take off any rings if you wear them. You will find if you use aromatherapy oils regularly that your nails strengthen and your hands become

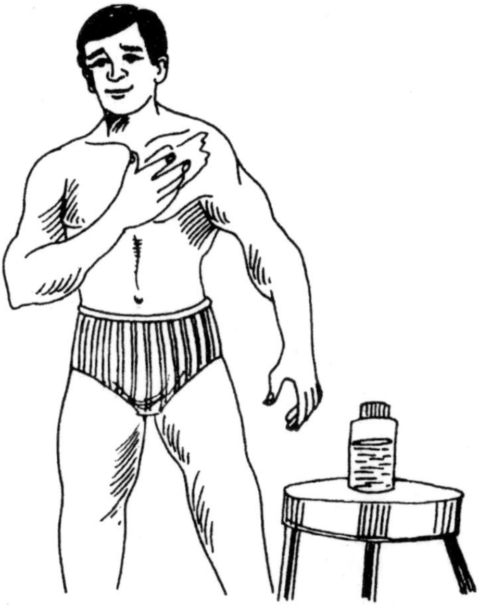

General Body Massage

smoother and more supple. Also, check with your massage partner to make sure there are no reasons to stop you going ahead.

THE FEET

Probably the most neglected part of our bodies, feet deserve a loving massage from time to time. Make sure your partner is warm and comfortable. Uncover one foot by folding back the towel or blanket. Now pour a little of your chosen oil into the palm of one hand. Rub your hands together to evenly distribute the oil. Now you are ready to begin.

❑ Enclose the foot between both hands (one on top, one underneath), then gently slide your hands off the foot coming forward to the toes. This movement should be slow and soothing. Repeat four or five times.

❑ Gently circle around the ankles using your thumbs. This area can be tender, so go easy.

❑ Rub over the top of the foot with your thumbs in little circles, coming down from the andkle area to the toes. Repeat three or four times.

❑ Now rub each toe with the same little circular movements.

❑ Rotate each toe twice in each direction.

❑ Gently pull each toe between finger and thumb.

❑ Zigzag down the sole of the foot from toes to heel with your thumbs overlapped.

❑ Enclose the foot in your hands then rub them in opposite directions, to create frictions. This is very warming.

❑ Hold the foot firmly and slowly rotate the ankle clockwise then anti-clockwise. Repeat a couple of times.

❑ Repeat step 1.

Once complete, wrap the foot up again for warmth and repeat the movements on the repeat the movements on the other foot. By now your massage partner will be feeling more relaxed and at ease with your touch.

THE LOWER LEGS AND KNEES

Warm a little oil in your hands.

❑ With one hand behind the other, smooth the oil on to the front of the leg, starting at the top of the foot and working up to the knee. This movement distributes the oil and soothes and relaxes the whole area.

❑ Rub acroos the front of the leg using both hands to create frictions. This increases the blood circulation to the area and reduces aches and pains.

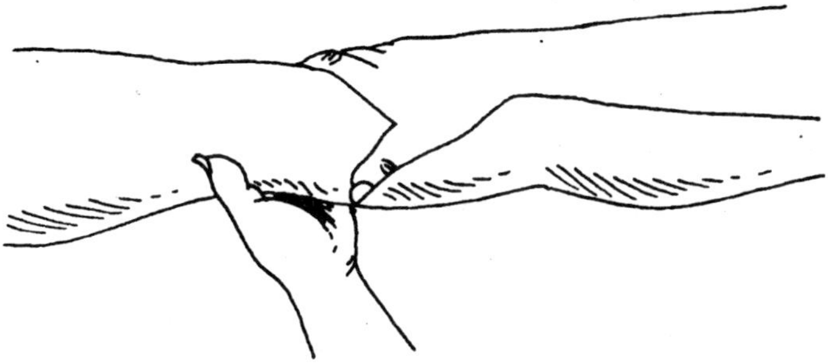

Massage on Leg

❑ Lift the leg up so the knee is bent. Squeeze and relax rhythmically down the muscles of the calf from knee to ankle. Repeat several times. Put the leg down.

❑ Work around the kneecap in little circular motions with both hands. Be careful not to use too much pressure.

❑ Now using your thumbs gently slide them around each side of the kneecap.

❑ Stretch out your thumbs from your fingers to create an arch. Sweep over the whole knee using alternate hands several times.

Now Wrap up the lower leg and proceed to the thigh.

THE UPPER LEGS

❑ Apply oil as for the lower leg.

❑ Glide up the leg from knee to groin, using one hand behind the other. This movement should be fairly slow and rhythmical. Make sure your movements cover the whole of the thigh area. Repeat four to five times.

❑ Stroke the upper inner thigh diagonally from knee to groin hand over hand. Repeat four or five times.

❑ Squeeze and release rhythmically first along the inner thigh from knee to groin, then along the outer thigh.

❑ Using your knuckles rake quickly up from the knee to the groin, taking in the whole thigh area. This is a friction movement and increases the surface blood circulation. You'll notice the skin colours quite quickly and feels warmer to the touch.

❑ Uncover the lower leg, then effleurage the whole leg from foot to groin as in step 2.

❑ Finish off by enclosing the foot in your hands a couple of times. Cover the leg then repeat all the movements on the other one.

By now you'll find your hands have become more sensitive to your partner and you'll notice differences in the skin texture and muscle tone.

THE HANDS AND ARMS

❑ Smooth on the oil as before. When working on the arm it's easier to effleurage with one hand only, using the other to hold the arm steady.

❑ Bend the arm at the elbow. Massage around the wrist with little thumb circles using both hands.

❑ Work down from the wrist to the ends of the fingers using little thumb circles. Repeat five times.

❑ Stretch each finger, then thumb, in turn between your finger and thumb.

❑ Rotate the fingers and thumb first clockwise then anti-clockwise.

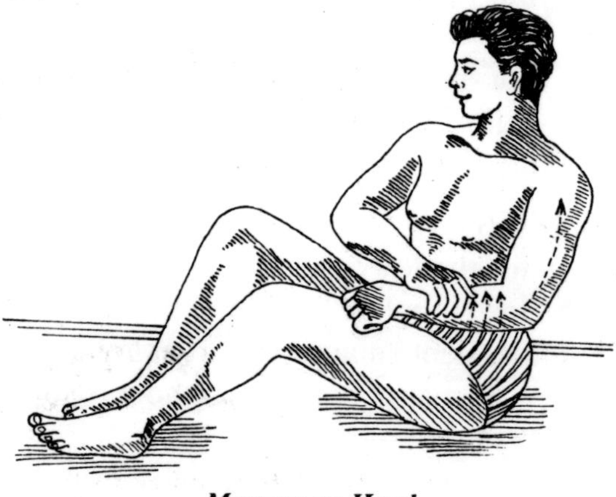

Massage on Hand

❑ Turn the hand over and rub gently along the solar plexus (from centre wrist down the palm to the middle finger) using alternate thumbs. This is calming to the nervours system.

❑ Rotate the hand at the wrist clockwise then anti-clockwise. To do this lock your fingers into your partner's.

❑ Turn the hand over and work on the inside of the wrist up to the elbow using alternate sweeping movements. Repeat four or five times.

❑ Bend the arm at the elbow and bring the lower arm up and across the chest. Squeeze all along the upper arm from elbow to shoulder using both hands.

❑ Bring the arm back down to the side then effleurage the whole area from hand to shoulder four or five times. Cover the arm and repeat on the other side.

THE ABDOMEN

The abdomen is a soft area protecting vital organs, so please be gentle. Fold the towel or blanket down to expose the area from just below the breasts to a couple of inches (centimetres) below the navel.

❑ Apply oil, starting just under the rib-cage, working down and out towards the waist. Be careful to keep your hands relaxed and contoured to your partner. Poking fingers feel very uncomfortable here.

❑ With one hand on top of the other iron around the lower abdomen in large circles. Keep the pressure light and even.

❑ Fan your hands out and work from the navel out to the waist. Slide your hands under the waist then gently pull them back round to the front again. Repeat several times.

❑ Stroke diagonally with alternate hands from the waist down to below the navel, first on the left side, then on the right.

❑ Stroke down from the solar plexus to the navel, one hand behind the other, to finish off this area.

THE BACKS OF THE LEGS

❑ Effleurage oil as for the front of the legs but working from the foot right up to the top of the thigh. Repeat four of five times.

❑ Bend the leg at the knee, supporting it with one hand. Stroke firmly down the calf, across behind the knee, then back up to the foot several times keeping your hands contoured to the leg. Put the leg down.

❑ Work up the calf to the knee, using little circles. Repeat several times to cover the whole calf.

❑ Using your index and middle fingers, make small circular movements behind the knee. Be careful not to press too hard.

❑ Squeeze rhythmically along the inner thigh from the knee upwards. Repeat on the outer thigh, doing each movement several times.

❑ Diagonally stroke from the inner knee upwards and across the thigh. Repeat several times.

❑ Finish by effeuraging the whole leg several times, from foot to thigh. Wrap up and repeat on the other leg.

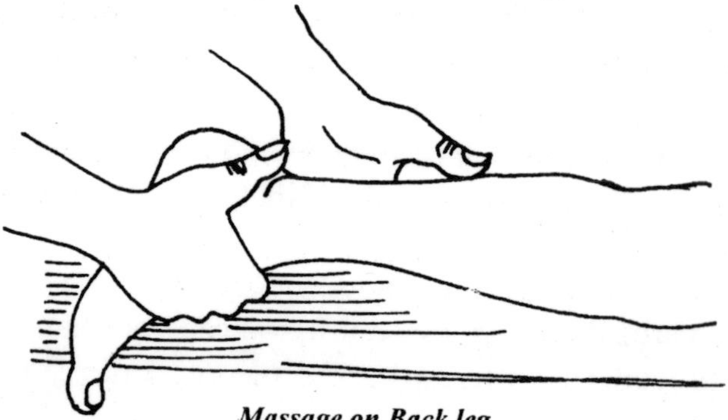

Massage on Back leg

THE BACK

Don't be at all surprised if your massage partner dozes off at this point. Back massage is extremely soothing and relaxing and great for relieving stress and tension.

Uncover the back to just show the buttock crease. At this point it is a good idea to place a small rolled-up towel under your partner's forehead otherwise he or she will have to turn his or her head sideways or end up with a squashed nose through which it is difficult to breathe.

❑ Starting at the lower back effleurage oil using both hands. Work slowly up the back to the shoulders, pressing gently on the upward strokes, releasing the pressure as you come back down.

❑ Starting at the base of the spine work up on either side, using gentle thumb pressure or little thumb circles. Repeat five or six times.

❑ With reinforced hands (one on top of the other) sweep up the spine then work around the shoulder blades in a figure-of-eight movement. Repeat the figure-of-eight four or five times.

❑ Now work around each shoulder blade individually, still with reinforced hands, in a circular motion. Repeat four of five times each side. You may feel knots (little bumps) around the shoulder blades. These are an indication of tension, and massage here gives great relief.

❑ Work around the shoulder blades with your thumbs, helping

to break down the knots and bumps. Allow your partner to be your guide as these areas can be tender.

❑ Squeeze along the top of the shoulders from the neck out, using your fingers and thumbs. Repeat four to five times on each side.

❑ Stroke up the back of the neck and out to the ears, using your thumbs.

❑ Stand at your partner's head and sweep your hands down the centre back, across the top of the buttocks, then firmly pull up at the sides. Repeat five times.

❑ Move to your partner's side and rub backwards and forwards over the whole back with frictions to warm the area.

❑ Make thumb circles out from just above the buttock crease round towards the hips. This area can often be tender and massage here is soothing. Repeat several times.

❑ Effleurage the whole back.

❑ Gently stroke up the spine, hand over hand, several times, allowing your touch to get lighter and lighter.

❑ Finish by gently holding your partner. Place one hand at the base of the spine, the other at the base of the neck. Hold this position and feel the warmth build up under your hands. After approximately one minute gently lift your hands off. Cover your partner over.

By now, he or she might be snoozing!

THE SHOULDERS AND NECK

If your partner is feeling very tense, and you haven't time to give a full body massage, working on the shoulders and neck will still offer great relief. For this your partner should be lying on his or her back. Uncover the chest by folding down the towel or blanket.

❑ Apply oil to your partner's chest, shoulders and neck.

❑ Begin effleuraging by placing both hands on the upper chest, fingers facing towards each other. Now, slowly pull your hands across the chest and out to the shoulders. Curve your hands round the shoulders and under them, then bring your hands in to meet at the back of the neck. Stroke up the neck to the base of the skull, Repeat four or five times.

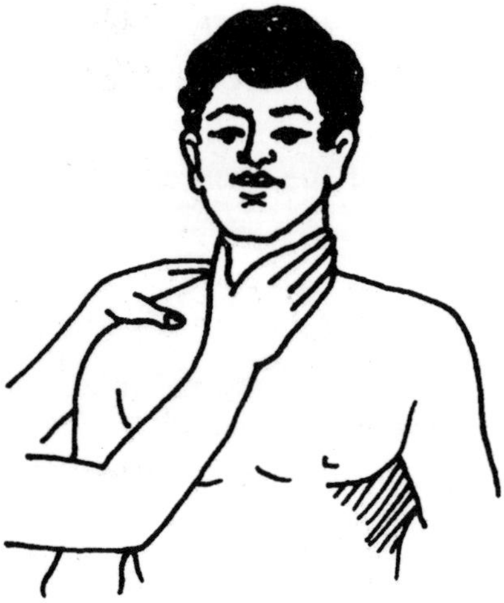

Massage of the neck

❑ Gently knuckle the chest and shoulders in the sequence shown in the diagram on the left. To knuckle make your hands into relaxed fists, and move the knuckles in circular movements. This sounds more difficult than it is.

❑ Gently turn your partner's head to one side. Stroke along the top of the shoulder and the side of the neck with your first three fingers. Repeat three times.

❑ Repeat the above sequence, but circle your fingers this time. Do this three times.

❑ Turn your partner's head to the other side and repeat movements 4 and 5. Return the head to the centre.

❑ Slide your hands down your partner's back as far as you can comfortably reach. Find the groove each side of the spine with your fingers. Pull your hands up the spine with a little pressure on the groove each side. Repeat three times.

❑ Now you are going to stretch the neck—these movements stretch out the muscles of the shoudlers and ncek and ease tension. If your partner is relaxed you'll find you will take all the weight of the head. If he or she is tense, go easy and make the movements slow and gentle. You don't want any pulled muscles.

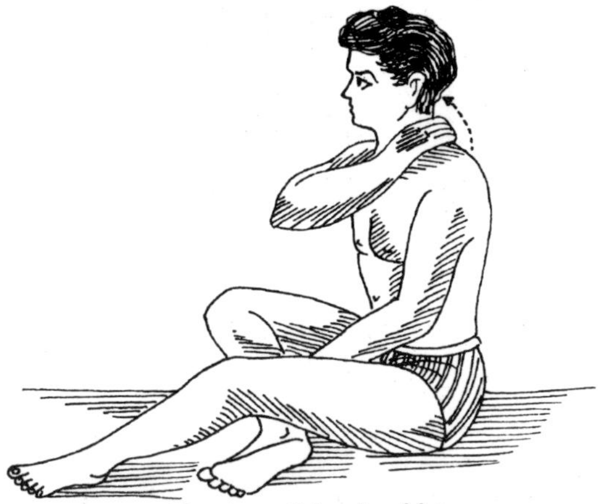

Massage of the shoulder

❑ Cup both hands unde your partner's head, your fingers resting in the base of the skull. Lift the head slightly, then gently pull towards you. Lower the head slowly, then repeat.

❑ Hold the back of the head in one hand and move it slowly towards the left shoulder while gently pressing down on the right shoulder with your other hand. Bring the head back to the centre and then repeat on the other side.

❑ Finish with some effleurage movements as you begin.

THE FACE AND SCALP

Until you've had the pleasurable experience of a face massage you probably won't have realized how much tension we hold in our faces. Think of frowning—this is caused by muscle action, and these muscles tire just as much as those of any other part of the body. A caring face massage can smooth away some of this tension, leaving us looking (and feeling) more at ease and relaxed.

Offer to take your partner's hair off the face with a headband, as it will inevitably get a little ouly around the hairline during the massage. Be careful not to use too much oil on the face or you'll find it difficult to massage specific areas without slipping.

Encourage your partner to close his or her eyes, so as to focus on your touch. Also, it can be disconcerting to have someone staring up at you, especially as a novice.

❑ Begin by stroking up each side of the jawline to the forehead. Repeat four or five times.

Massage of face

❑ Slowly stroke the forehead rhythmically with the flat of your hand from just above the brows to the hairline.

❑ Starting at the centre hairline slide your thumbs out to the side, applying gentle pressure. Move down the forehead slightly and repeat. Continue this outward stroking pressure until you reach the eyebrows.

❑ Now place the heel of each hand on the centre forehead and slide out to the sides. Repeat three times.

❑ Place the first two fingers of each hand on the temples and circle gently for a minute or two, applying a little pressure.

All the above movements help to relieve a headache. Try lavender oil for your massage, as I've found it can ward off a headache if used in time.

❑ Place your thumbs on your partner's inner eyebrows and slide out to the sides. Repeat three times.

❑ With your index finger and thumb gently pull along the brow bone. Repeat three times.

❑ Stroke gently over the eyelids with your ring fingers, from the inner to the outer conrners. Repeat three times.

❑ Alternately stroke down the nose with your thumbs, then gently rub round the nose tip and nostrils. Be careful not to press hard on the nostrils.

❑ Stroke the cheeks across the cheekbones and gradually work down the face to the chin.

❑ Make little circular movements across the top lip. When you reach the corner of the mouth lift slightly, then repeat.

❑ Make pinching movements out along the jawline and up towards the ears.

❑ Rub the earlobes between your fingers and thumb, then gently pinch all around the outer ear. Most people love this.

❑ Sweep your hands up the neck and on to the cheeks. Hold, then repeat.

❑ Finish by stroking the forehead, getting lighter and lighter until you bring your hands off.

SCALP MOVEMENTS

❑ Remove your partner's headband. Bring your hands up the side of the face to the forehead, then rake them through the hair. Repeat several times.

❑ 'Glue' your fingers onto the scalp and move it around against the skull. Move your fingers to a different position and repeat this process until all the scalp has been covered.

❑ Rub vigorously over the scalp, as if shampooing the hair.

❑ Take little bunches of hair all over the scalp and tug gently. This feels lovely and really stimulates the scalp.

❑ Repeat step 1 to finish off.

❑❑

18

WONDERFUL TREATMENT THERAPY—*SHIRODHARA*

Shirodhara means to pure medicated oil on head in a stream.

Now-a-days the problems of headace, high blood pressure, heart diseases, grey hair, etc. are very common. Financial, professional, social and family problems affect human life much. A tired body and aching limbs crave for attention at the end of day's hard work or after a long journey. At this time a hot or cold bath depending on the weather conditions brings great relief to them. But there is also another way to relieve such aches and pains. It is through massage and pressure. *Shirodhara* technique is a part of it.

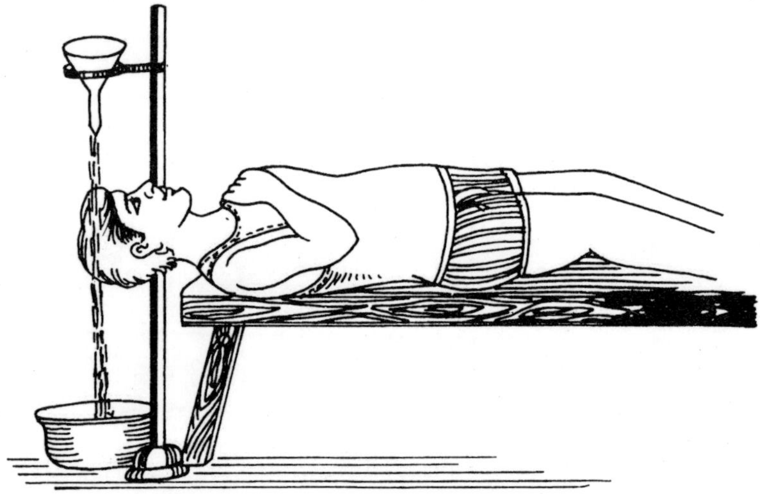

Shirodhara is a wounderful treatment theraphy

In ayurveda, much importance was given to oil massage to protect health. The parts of a machine are oiled to work properly.

In the same way the organs of the body require massage with oil to assist in their functions properly. Massage on head is much important as the mind controls all the organs of the body and then functions. Oil massage helps in the functions of the mind. It has been developed in *Shirodhara*. Mind and soul, which make a man active, reside in human brain according to ayurved. Brain is their work-spot. It is the brain which controls all the functions of the body. *Shirodhara* is the best technique to keep the mind healthy.

METHOD

The body of the patient is massaged with oil at first. Then the patient is laid on a special table made for *Shirodhara*. *Shirodhara* is poured on his forehead and head. His eyes covered with cotton pads.

A special pot is made to keep oil. This pot is broad on the above side and small on the lower side. There is a small hole in the bottom of the pot. If this pot is made of gold, iron or earth its effect is better. Now-a-days is iron or copper pots are used more. This pot is tied with a strong string 4 to 5 inches above the head of the patient lying on the table.

Now the pot is filled with medicated oil and its stream starts falling over the head of the patient. The stream of oil should fall over the mid of forehead of the patient. An attendant standing nearby takes special care of it. The falling oil over the forehead passes through a pipe and it is collected in a pot kept under the table for this purpose. This oil is again poured in the pot tied above the head of the patient. The process of *Shirodhara* should not be discontinued before time.

OIL FOR *SHIRODHARA*

Medicines and oil are selected according to the diseases and nature of the patient. Ayurvedic medicines and herbs are boiled in mustard or til oil. This oil is used for *Shirodhara*.

Oil prepared with *Dashmool* medicines is used in *Vat* problems and oil prepard with *Majeeth* and *Anantmool* medicines is used in Pitta problems.

TIME FOR *DHARA*

It should be done in morning hours. The patient should take rest for sometime after the process.

Benefits : *Shirodhara* pacifies brain and mind. It strengthens the senses. The seses and the mind work through the brain. The best way to improve the health of the mind, brain and senses is *Shirodhara.*

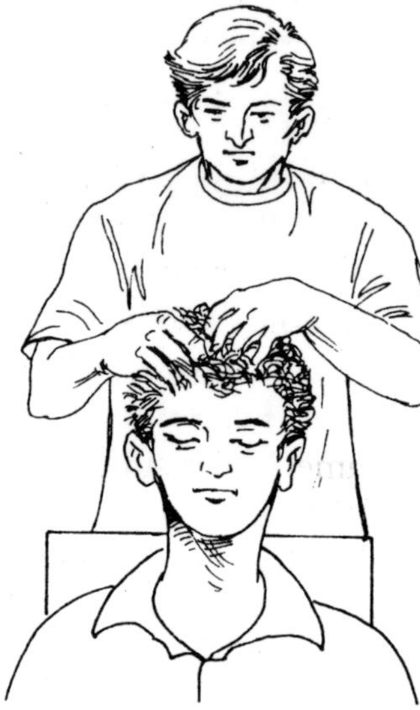

Massage of head

Its effects are good in relieving headache and Vat problems. Hearing power, voice and eyesight are improved by it. Tension, discomfort, despair, anger, depression, sadmess and other mental agonies disturb the balance of the Vat which results in headache, greying of hair, falling of hair, insomnia, etc. *Shirodhara* is the best treatment has been adopted by a majority of patients in Kerala. Foreigners visit Kerala every year in large number to get relief in their diseases by *Shirodhara* and other techniques of massage.

❑❑

19

OILS AND HERBS FOR DIFFERENT DISEASES

Oils and herbs which are available at home are effective for preparing massage oil and they cure several diseases. They cost very little when compared to commercial preparations. They are as follows:

❑ Mustard oil ❑ Sesame oil ❑ Camphor oil ❑ Eucalyptus oil ❑ Almond oil ❑ Olive oil ❑ Coconut oil ❑ Castor oil ❑ Herbs available in kitchen

RESPIRATORY PROBLEMS

❑ Add camphor powder to coconut oil and heat it slightly. It gives relief in common cold, rattling phelgm in the chest and cough.

❑ It should be rubbed on the nose for common cold. It should be rubbed on the throat for throat cough and on chest for chest cough.

❑ If the nose is blocked, massage with two or three drops of mustard oil on the nose.

ASTHMA, BRONCHITIS

Take two spoons of garlic juice and mix it in half a cup of til oil. Heat the oil till the juice evaporates. Remove it from fire. Cool and store it in a bottle. Heat it before use and massage on the chest.

DIGESTIVE PROBLEMS

Pain in Stomach and Constipation

Heat castor oil slightly and massage it around and above the navel. It will give relief in stomach cramps and pain and remove constipation.

Flaulence and Fullness

Add a pinch of Asafoetida powder in til oil or mustard oil. Heat it slightly and rub on the abdomen.

SKIN DISEASES

Add dry curry leaves to coconut oil and keep it in the sun for 15 days. Massage this oil on the skin two hours before bath. This cures and prevents any type of itching and eruption. It gives bright glow to the skin and makes it healthy.

ARTHRITIS AND RHEUMATISM

❑ If the pain is mild and tolerable, massage mustard oil on the affected part.

❑ Powder Ajwain and extract oil from it. Massage the painful joints with oil.

❑ Add 10 to 15 cloves to 4 table spoons of til oil and heat. When the garlic becomes black, remove it from fire and add one spoon camphor powder. Rub this oil three to four times a day.

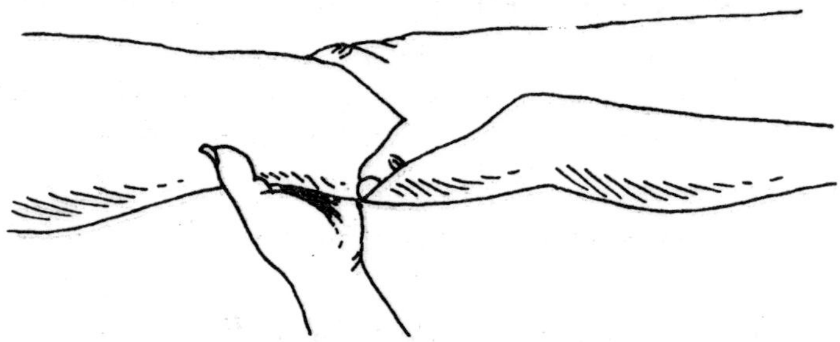

In rheumatism pain rub oil over affected joint

❑ If the pain is chronic with inflammation, the herbal oil should be prepared as following:

- 200 gm til oil
- 1 spoon of Ajwain
- 1 spoon of cloves
- 8 garlic pieces. Peel them and crush them.
- 2 spoons mustard seeds.

Heat oil and add mustard seeds to splutter. Powder Ajwain and cloves. Add all these ingredients to the oil and stir well. The garlic should turn black. Remove it from fire, cool and store in a bottle. Rub this oil on the affected joints.

SPINAL MASSAGE

❑ Massage must not be given on the bones of spine directly but two inches from the centre. Massage on either side of spine assists in curing the organs of the front side of the body.

❑ Divide the back into upper and lower divisions. Massage on either side of the spine on the upper division to treat diseases of lungs, heart, stomach, liver and other digestive organs. Massage either side of spine on the lower division to cure the diseases of the kidneys, intestines, urinary and menstrual problems.

BENEFICIAL PROPERTIES OF MUSTARD OIL

Mustard oil is used frequently in our country India. It is often used in cooking food. Massage with mustard oil is most prevalent in India. Use of pure yellow mustard oil is considered the best. Mustard oil contains various properties which are effective in curing diseases.

Mustard oil is used in our daily life in the following ways:

❑ Its massage in the body gives energy and strength. The bones of the body become strong.

❑ Warm the mustard oil with garlic. When garlic becomes black, remove it from the fire, cool it and massage it on the body of a child. This prescription has a curative effect.

❑ Mix the powdered salt with the mustard oil. Rub it on the teeth. It cleanses the teeth and gives relief in pain. Some persons use it daily to cleanse the teeth.

- ❑ If hand and feet are aching, massage with mustard oil.
- ❑ Massage with mustard oil on head relieves headache.
- ❑ If there is dirt and filth in the ear and it is aching, pour some drops of lukewarm mustard oil. It will relieve the pain soon.
- ❑ If the hand and feet are rough and dry, massage lightly with mustard oil. Massage with mustard oil cures dryness and the skin becomes soft.
- ❑ If you are too tired, warm the mustard oil with garlic and massage the soles with it, you will be relaxed beyond expectation.
- ❑ The fingers of the feet become tender by working continuously in water. Regular massage of them with mustard oil cures them.
- ❑ After massage, one should take sunbath for sometime in winter season. It gives glow to the skin and the bones become stong. One should take bath after half an hour of sunbath.

❑❑

20

PRODUCTION METHOD OF ESSENTIAL OILS

There are many methods to extract the aromatic qualities from plants. Teas, tinctures, decoctions, infused oils, herbal beers, and wines all extract and concertrate the volatile components of the plants but these are not essential oils. Essential oils are much more concentrated, and are produced by steam distillation, cold pressing, CO_2 hyperbaric extraction, and solvent extraction. Each method has its advantages and disadvantages and produces a different quality of oil.

Steam distillation is the most common method of essential oil extraction.

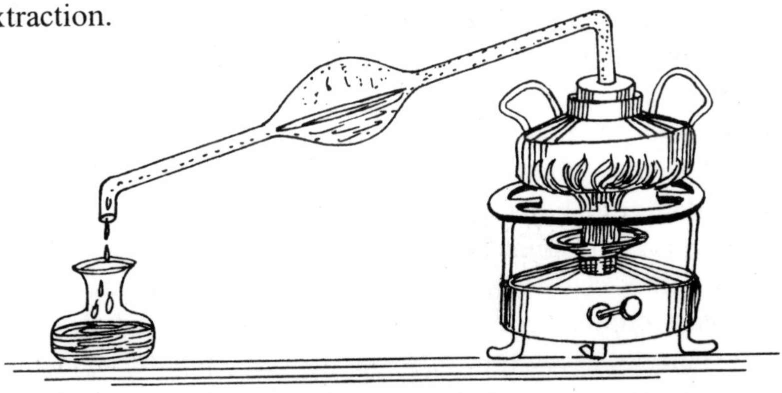

A filteration method

Distillation uses the extraction abilities of steam, and sometimes pressure, to pull the plant material is placed on screens over boiling water, or super-heated steam from another source is piped through the plant material. As the steam passes through the plant material, the volatile components are lifted, condensed in a cooling coil, and precipitate out as a combination of distilled water and volatile components. The mixture is collected in a florentine vase (which has an hourglass shape) and in most cases the distilled water is heavier and sinks to the bottom, while the essential oils, being lighter, reise to the top, at which point a valve can be opened and the essential oils drained off.

There are very primitive methods of steam distillation that use very low heat and may take as long as a month to distill one batch of essential oils. The advantage in 'slow' distillation is that the long time (and patience) allow some of the larger molecules to be gently coaxed out, and can produce an essence which has a wider range of smells. More moderm methods of distillation may use higher temperatures to very quickly extract essential oils, sometimes in a matter of minutes. This can produce oils quickly, cheaply and efficiently; however, the bouquet, or range of smells, is somewhat restricted by this method, and involves a loss in some of the possible therapeutic qualities.

Cold pressing is the second most common method of essential oil production and is most useful in the processing of citrus rinds such as lemon, orange, grapefruit, tangerine, bergamot and mandarin. The rinds, or in some cases the whole fruit, are chopped or ground, and pressed to extract the essential oil components that are found in the skin of the fruit. In early days, and in some places in the world today, the rinds of these fruits were squeezed into sponges. Take a piece of citrus rind, fold it, skin out, and notice the spray of essential oils (watch your eyes). Do this into a candle flame and witness the flash of blue as the volatiles ignite.

Cold pressing produces a combination of essential oils and watery components which can be allowed to separate and the essential components collected. The mechanical nature of this process produces essential oils which are not as pure, and tend to exidize or lose their potency if left unrefrigerated for more than two years. Steam-distilled essential oil, on the other hands, will grow richer in smell over the years and in some cases have unlimited shelf life.

The CO_2 hyperbaric production method utilizes as much as 22 atmospheres of pressure in the presence of pure CO_2 gas (the same pressure found at ocean depths of 660 feet). At high pressure the CO_2 becomes liquid and has the ability to extract the essential oil components from the plant material. This liquid is drained off and allowed to depressurize, at which point the CO_2 becomes a harmless gas. What's left in the bottom of the chamber is pure essential oil. This method is especially useful in some of the lighter fragrances such as tuberose or jasmine where the flowers have light, easily lost aromatic components. The cost of the compression equipment is great and oils produced are more expensive than steam distilled.

The solvent extraction method is also useful with light aromatic flowers. The flowers are collected and a solvent such as hexane or ether poured over them. The solvents are evaporated using a vacuum, and what's left as a very thick, sticky residuce known as a 'concrete'. The concrete can be dissolved in alcool, the alcohol pulled off, and the remaining essential oil be known as an 'absolute'. Perfumers like this mehtod because it doesn't involve heat, pressure, or mechanical pressing which can change to odor of the flowers. Perfumers maintain that absolutes are more true to the original smell of the flower than oils produced using any other method of production. Aromatherapists, however, know that a small amount of the petroleum solvent always remains, and can be harmful to the human immune system, causing reactions in sensitive people. In aromatherapy, it is the method least preferred, and oils produced in the manner are never used internally.

❑ ❑

21

OTHER PROCEDURES ADOPTED WITH AROMATHERAPY

Mud pack, genital bath, sponging, sunbath, fasting, deep breathing etc. are important procedures. Here I have described these procedure because one should know about these procedures along with Aroma Therapy.

MUD PACKS

The best way to prepare a mud pack is to take clay from about four inches below the surface of the earth. Ensure that the clay does not contain any impurities, like compost or pebbles. If there are any pebbles grind the clay and pass it through a sieve. Mix it with cold water and see that it has a consistency like soft dough. It should stick and not be thin enough to slide down when used in

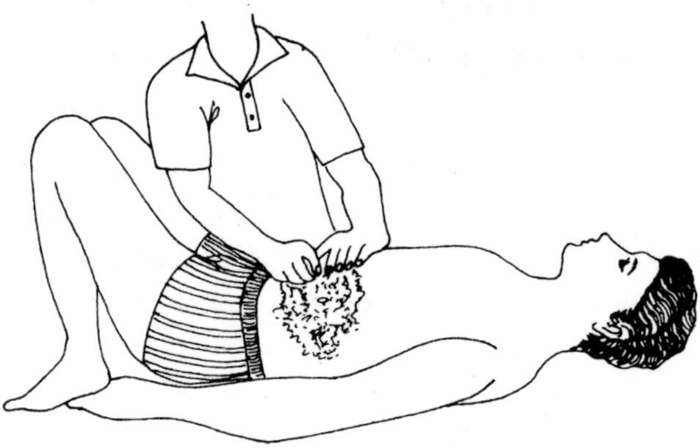

Method of using Mud Pack

the pack. If the pack is to be applied on the abdomen (from the navel to the pubes) spread the mud evenly on a piece of cloth.

See that it is about half an inch thick. Then place it gently with the cloth up and the mud touching the skin. Remove the cloth and place a thick wollen piece of cloth on the mud. You may even let the cotton cloth remain over the mud, but cover it with a thick woollen. If that is done the patient can keep lying down without covering himself with a blanket or a sheet.

The mud pack should be used for 20 to 30 minutes. After it is removed, clean the skin using a soft piece of cloth dipped in cold water.

Clay is to be found in different shades in different places, but whatever the colour, it is equally beneficial. If the mud is loamy and has a tendency to stikc to the skin, some sand can be mixed with it.

GENITALS BATH

Keep a stool one foot long, six inches wide and six inches high in the tub. It would be all the better if there is a circular cut in front of it. If a stool is not readily available keep four bricks, two upon two to raise the level and sit on them. The water level in the tub should be such that it is one inch above the stool. The water should be cold; during summer the water of an earthen pitcher can be used for the purpose.

Take off your clothes and sit on the stool. Take a piece of cloth, dip it in water and gently rub your abdomen with it for two minutes. Then take hold of the foreskin of your penis in two fingers and rub it lightly with a soft piece of cloth dipping cold water often. This can be continued for ten to twenty minutes. A lean person can do it for only ten minutes, and the hefty one for as long as twenty minutes. After the rubbing of the foreskin is completed, rub the entire spine with a wet towel for two minutes. You can take hold of the wet towel in two hands and move it up and down on your spine.

Women should rub their abdomen. They should take a piece of soft cloth, pull up the lips of the vagina and rub them slowly. And in the end they should also rub the spine as above. No hip bath or genitals bath should be taken at the time of menstruation.

You must take exercise, walk or lie down in a bed and wrap

yourself in a blanket to restore the body heat lost due to immersion in water.

If a tub is not available, this bath can be taken in the sun. In that case spread a wet towel on the stool on which you sit. Keep a bucket full of water near the stool and take the bath as indicated above.

HIP BATH

You must have seen specially made tubs for hip baths. The tub is oval in shape and one end of it is raised so that the patient can rest his back against it. This is the ideal tub for taking a hip bath.

Fill the tub with cold water. The level of the water should be so adjusted that it touches your navel when you sit in it. Your feet will be outside the tub and you can support them by keeping a low stool in front of the tub. You can rest your back against the raised portion of the tub and remain in that half supine position.

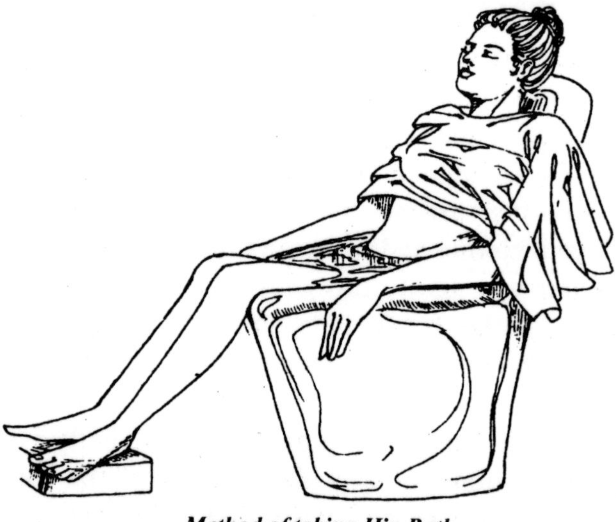

Method of taking Hip Bath

Take a rough towel and rub your abdomen from the right to the left. Do it gently so that the skin is not scraped. Do not apply too much pressure in rubbing.

A hip bath can be taken from ten to twenty minutes. Thin persons should take it for only ten minutes and the stout ones can continue for 20 minutes. During winter the duration of the hip bath should be reduced by about 25 per cent.

In the begining, the hip bath should be taken only for a minute or two; the time should be increased gradually to ten or twenty minutes, as indicated above.

If it is too cold, rub your body with your palms for five to seven minutes before getting into the tub. A vigorous rubbing of the body will bring warmth to it and you will not experience any discomfort when you start the hip bath.

Wipe your body with a towel when you get out of the tub, dress quickly and go for a walk or take some other exercise. Those too weak to engage in any such activity should get into bed and wrap a blanket around them and rest for half an hour to bring back warmth to their body.

You can take a bath a couple of hours after the hip bath and not before.

HOW TO TAKE A BATH

A bath is a daily ritual, but few people understand its purpose or importance. That is why most of us merely throw water over our heads and the bodies and think that we have done our duty. Throwing water over the body is beneficial but it is not what a bath is.

The twin purposes of a bath are: cleanliness and reactivating the circulation of the blood by the tingling sensation that cold water produces as it comes into contact with the skin. The first purpose, i.e. cleanliness, can be better served by hot water. The skin of the body has millions of pores through which the skin breathes as we do through our lungs. If the pores are clogged, the lungs are overworked. Overwork may lead to fatigue or exhaustion of the lungs. And then, closed pores do not pass any perspiration which the skin breathes as we do through our lungs. If the pores are clogged, the lungs are overworked.Overwork may lead to fatigue or exhaustion of the lungs. And then, closed pores do not pass any perspiration which is a must to clear the blood of morbid humours. Closed pores are a danger to the general health of human beings.

Cold water is also a cleansing agent, but it cannot deal with the grease and dirt infesting the pores of the skin. Hot water mixed with lemon juice is the best cleansing agent for the skin. Or, better still, take a lemon and roast it lightly over a fire. Then cut it into two parts, dip a part in hot water and rub it over your skin. This will cleanse your skin as no soap can do. But a hot bath should not be taken daily. It generally brings lethargy, weakness and slows down the digestive processes. Once or twice a week is enough if you have to take a hot bath. The temperature of the water should not be more than one or two degree above body temperature.

Indian bathing style

A hot bath before retiring for the night is the best for your health. It helps you to sleep better and if you cover your body after a hot bath, it will save you from the danger of exposure. A bath, hot or cold should be taken one hour before meals or three hours after it.

Really hot water for a bath has its own advantages but it should be used sparingly. If you are suffereing from a cold, take a hot bath, cover yourself with woollens and get into bed. It will drive away the cold. A really hot bath when you are tired acts as a tonic: it drives away fatigue as nothing else does.

A bath with hot water has its used, but a daily bath should be with cold water. When the skin is cooled by the cold water, blood rushes to warm it up. The circulation of the blood is activated and the blood is also cleansed of many impurities. A slowed down circulation is a prelude to old age. A cold bath is, therefore, instrumental in keeping us young.

The best way to start a bath is to rub the whole of your body with your palms or with a rough towel. Start with your scalp , forehead, face and the neck . Then go on to your wrists and then to the shoulders through the arms. Afterwards rub your chest, the armpits and abdomen and the back. The feet should be the lst to receive attention. Keep your feet straight when you rub them. Start from the feet and come upto the thighs. In the begining, rub gently but later increase the pressure.

After the vigorous rubbing, take a cold bath. Wipe your body with a towel. Start with the head and then dry up the whole body. You will feel a peculiar kind of pleasure when you rub your body afte a bath. For weak persons a rubbing can do the job of exercise.

If this method of taking a bath is adopted, there will not be any danger of any skin eruptions or itch. The face will be free of pimples and other blemishes which mar its beauty. The skin will acquire a healthy glow and if it is rough and leathery, it will become pink and soft. You will have the feeling as if you had been having an oil massage.

If the palms of the hand are used to dry up the body after a bath instead of a towel, it will be doubly beneficial. It gives pleasant sensation during winter.

WET PACK FOR THE WAIST

The bandage to be used as a wet pack for the waist should be seven to eight feet long and six inches broad. It should be of soft cotton cloth. Dip it in cold water, ring it lightly and wrap it around your waist. It should cover the area from the navel to a little above the pubes and should remain in direct contact with the skin. Cover the wet bandage with a woollen cloth of equal dimensions and secure with a safety pin or a string so that it does not loosen up.

There will be a cold sensation on the skin covered by the wet pack but after about ten minutes warmth will return. If you still feel cold after ten minutes, that is an indication that the bandage has been wrapped lightly and has to be tightend. Or, the bandage has not been properly wrung out or it is thicker than it should be.

The wet pack for the waist can be used from half an hour to two hours at a time.

WET PACK FOR THE CHEST

The dimensions of the bandage for the chest should be the same as for the waist. It should be similarly dipped in cold water, wrung out and wrapped round the chest and covered by a woollen piece of cloth. It should be wrapped in such a way that it should cover the chest, the upper part of the shoulders and the corresponding portion of the back. The woollen covering for the wet pack should be secured with a safety pin or a piece of string as in the case of the waist pack.

This pack can also be used for half an hour to two hours.

SUN BATH

Sun bath is an important tool of the naturopath. Even though people in the west use it for cosmetic purposes, it plays an important part in restoring health.

In Indian conditions, the ideal times for a sun bath during summer is 6-6.30 in the morning and during winter from 7-7.30.

Take off all your clothes and sit in a secluded corner away from interruptions. The whole of your body should be exposed to the health-giving rays of the sun.

In the beginning take a sun bath for only two to three minutes but increase the timing gradual to fefteen to twenty minutes.

When the sunlight is very hot, cover your head with a towel. If you cannot find a secluded place to take the sun bath, cover yourself with a light cotton sheet.

SUN-BATH FOR INDUCING PERSPIRATION

Sweat can be induced through a sun bath. For this purpose the sun is hot enough at ten to eleven in the morning in summer and two to three in the afternoon in winter. Take hot water and lie down naked on a mattress or blanket spread on the floor. If the wind is strong, chose a place in the lee of the wind.

You will start sweating in about ten to fifteen minutes after you have lied down. After fifteen to twenty minutes, whether you sweat or not, you must take a cold bath just after it.

Some people may not perspire in the begining but after repeating the sun bath for three of four days, their sweat glands will be activated and they will perspire.

You must cover you head with a wet towel while taking a sun bath, but at the same time go on sipping warm water to aid the body to produce the sweat.

SPONGING THE BODY

When you are running a temperature, a sponge bath is more advisable than a bath. The patient should be covered with a sheet or blanket and his body should be wiped with a wet towel. Wipe his feet first, one after the other. Rub them with the wet towel for four to five minutes and then wipe them with a dry towel. But even when the feet have been dried rub them with the palms of the hand so that some heat is generated in the body. In the case of fever, such rubbing is not advised.

Sponging the body

After the feet have been attended to go to the calves and the rest of the legs, the abdomen, the chest, the back, the face and the neck. The hands should be rubbed for five to six minutes and the abdomen, chest and the back a little longer.

The total time taken for a sponge bath is on an average half an hour. The ideal time for a sponge bath is mid day.

FASTING

Nothing but water should be taken when you are fasting. The intake of water must be two to two and a half litres. One feels fresh if one continues drinking water and the intake of water also helps the expulsion of morbid matter from the body.

In the evening of the first day of the fast and the morning after, an enema of hot water should be taken to clean the bowels.

One day's fasting should be followed by a food intake 25% less than one normally takes. A two days fast should be followed by ingestion of fruits only the next day; normal food should follow the next day. A three day's fast should be followed the next day by fruit juices and soup of vegetables (the soup must be clear, without addition of any thickening agents or condiments). On the fifth day eat fruits only and on the sixth breakfast on fruits, lunch on bread and boiled vegetables and repeat a fruit diet for your dinner. It is only after wards that you should resume your normal diet.

FRUITS, FRUIT JUICES AND MILK DIETS

When you have been advised to live on fruit juices or juices or soups of vegetables, you should take sbout 250 millilitres of fruit juice or juice or clear soup of a vegetable three to four times in the day. The best juices are those of oranges pineapple, rose apple, raspberry and tomatoes. If the juice is too thick, mix it with plain water in the proportion of 1:¾th.

Juice of gourd, tomatoes and carrot can be taken in its natural form. If you do not have a juicer (a machine to extract the juice of fruits) grate the fruits or vegetables and sqeeze then through fine muslin or other fine meshed cloth.

Other vegetables have to be half a kilogramme and should be boiled in 250 millilitres of water and the juice drunk.

When you are living on fruit, take them thrice daily. But take one kind of fruit at one meal. For example, you can take tomatoes for breakfast, oranges at lunch time and apples for your dinner. If you can take the same fruit at all meal times, it would be still better.

The total intake of fruits in the day should not be more than one to one and a half kilogrammes.

When a diet of fruit and milk is indicated, take 250 to 300 millilitres of milk with the fruits. If your appetite improves, as it should the quantity of the milk can be increased to half a litre at one time. Unboiled milk should be taken in the morning and even during lunch time milk boiled in the morning can be ingested. Sip the milk as you munch the fruit. It will be more beneficial than eating the fruit and drinking the milk.

Even when you are on a diet of fruit juices, do not forget to drink one to two litres of water in the day. If your bowels do not move automatically during the fruit and milk diet, take recourse to an enema. But the bowels must be evacuated properly and no morbid humours or substances should be allowed to accumulate in the body.

INTAKE OF WATER

One must drink one to one and a half litres of water in 24 hours. The best time for taking water is the first thing in the morning, one hour before meals and two hours after. If you must drink water during the meals, see that the quantity does not exceed 200 to 250 millilitres. If you have taken water one hour before the meals, you will not feel the need to take it during eating. But still, water may be taken during the meal according to need and inclination.

WALKING

During a walk, you must move briskby. Your back should be straight and the arms moving.

The normal speed of walking should be about four miles per hour. Take a different route for a walk every day as that would be more enjoyable instead of taking the same route every day.

Five to six miles walk in the morning and two to three miles in the evening is the best. Those who are starting to take a walk should not overstrain themselves but increases the distance gradually.

DEEP BREATHING

Deep breaths should be taken during a walk. Inhalation should become a natural rhythm with you. Inhalation andexhalation should not be done slowly.

SLEEP

Sleep should be sufficient to give a sense of relief from exhaustion. But do not oversleep, nor laze about in bed when you are not sleeping. The ideal time for sleep is from 9 o'clock in

the night to 5 in the morning. Those who feel sleepy all the time return to normal sleeping hours after some days.

During summer, a siesta for an hour or so will refresh you. If you cannot sleep, relax for an hour after lunch.

INHALATION AND VAPORISATION

Inhalations are considered to be highly effective, as the olfactory (smelling) receptors have direct links with the brain. Inhalations are said to quite useful and effective in routing skin-care treatment, respiratory conditions, such as colds, coughs, sore throats, catarrh, blocked nasal passages but use with utmost care if you are an asthmatic, Vaporisers and scented baths can also prove relaxing and invigorating, depending on the oil chosen for a specific physical/mental problems.

For inhalations add 4 drops of a suitable essential oil to a bowl of steaming water and then lean over the bowl with you head covered by a towel but keep your eyes closed . Breathe in deeply. Initially, inhalation may be a bit problematic but once the blocked and stuck up nostritls are cleared of trapped muslces, inhalation will automatically improve.

You can use eucalyptus or peppermint oil (4-6 drops or either or 2-3 drops of each of the oils). If steam inhalation is not feasible, you can put 4-5 drops of the oil on a hanky (tissue cloth) hold it to your nose and take deep breathes. But do not inhale directly from the bottle itself.

❑❑

22

POOL THERAPY AND MEDICATED BATHS

Doing certain exercises after immersing the body in deep water is called pool therapy. It is very effective for management of painful conditions such as arthritis and contraction of the muscles.

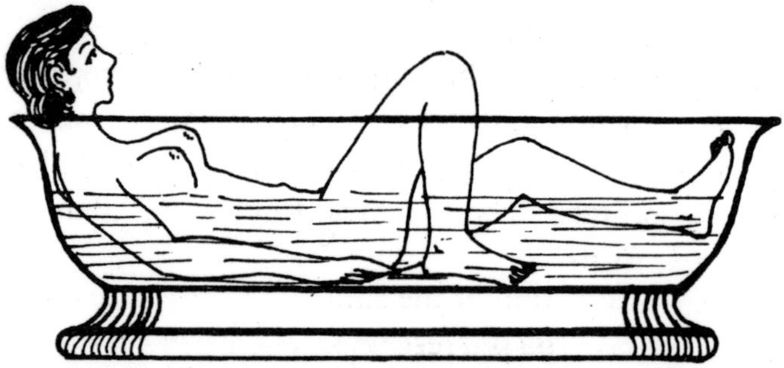

Pool therapy is often used for management of poliomyelitis and spastic muscles at a rehabilitation centre. In these pools, you can walk a few steps and perform various movements of hips, back, upper back, hands, shoulders and the legs. The main advantage of doing exercises in water is that due to the buoyancy you can do movements of the affected part more easily than on the ground.

WHAT ARE MEDICATED BATHS?

Having bath in water to which medicinal substances are added is called medicated bath. These substances include, among others, common salt, sulphur, mustard powder, foam forming extracts, pine extracts, alkaline bath, sea weed and some antiseptics.

Medicated baths are effective because they act as counter irritant and antiseptics. They also increase buoyancy of the immersed body. There are several types of medicated baths. These include:

Brine bath : Artificial brine bath is prepared by adding two and a half to three kilograms of common salt to a bath tub filled with warm water. The temperature of the water is maintained between 90-105°F or as much as you can tolerate.

Brine bath stimulates the skin and therefore results in profuse sweating. After having the brine bath, a blanket is often wrapped around the body to continue sweating. Brine bath is normally recommended for management of some skin diseases and rheumatism. Having bath in sea water has effects similar to a brine bath.

Sulphur bath : In this bath, 150 to 250 grams of potash with sulphur is added to a bath tub filled with water. The temperature of the water ranges from 90-102°F. A sulphur bath is usually recommended for 10 to 20 minutes to manage skin infections, pimples, skin infestations and some skin eruptions.

Mustard bath : This bath is given by adding 850 to 900 and grams of mustard to a bath tub filled with water at a temperature of 96-100°F. Mustard bath is recommended for 10 to 15minutes. The oil in the mustard results in irritation of skin and therefore enhances the effect of a plain immersion bath. This irritation increases blood circulation of the skin.

Spa treatment : A spa is a resort that has a natural spring with some chemicals that have medicinal properties. A mineral spring used for spa treatment has a higher mineral content as compared to normal drinking water and/or its temperature is above 20°C.

The type of diseases that can be managed by spa treatment depends on the mineral content of the water in it. In recent times, the use of spa have either become tourist attractions or are used for relaxation purposes.

It is important to remember that the use of water for management of various diseases in its various forms has several advantages and contraindication. It is therefore important that you avoid using water treatment without direct supervision of a trained Nature Cure practitioner. Some of these treatments can result in severe adverse effects if not used properly.

❑❑

23

AROMATHERAPY AND SPA TREATMENTS

Facials, peels, hair removal, body massages, and body treatments are on most spa menus. The fundamentals of the services are similar in all spas, while signature treatments, products used, and personalized methods make each spa unique. Guests

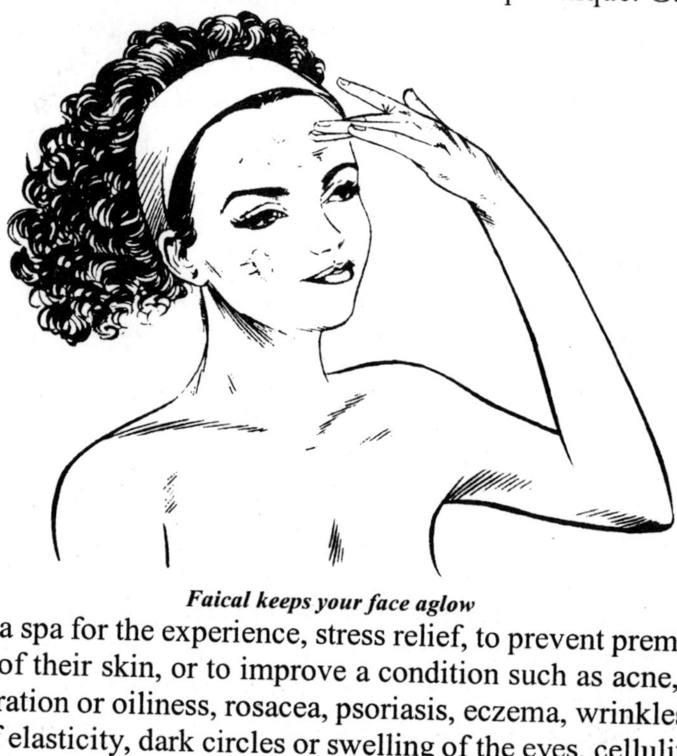

Faical keeps your face aglow

select a spa for the experience, stress relief, to prevent premature aging of their skin, or to improve a condition such as acne, skin dehydration or oiliness, rosacea, psoriasis, eczema, wrinkles and loss of elasticity, dark circles or swelling of the eyes, cellulite, or heavy legs, Pre-and post-operative care reduces swelling, bruising and discomfort.

FACIALS

Facials are the most popular service in spas. The facials introduced in America by European estheticians since the early 1900s have been commonly termed "European facials." They are cleansing facials, different from skin treatments. Facials take approximately an hour and include an exfoliation, a massage, steam or a warm towel application, extraction of comedones, a mask, and the application of a serum, ampoule, or essential oils. A treatment consists of the use of equipment, a specialty massage, or a mask. The esthetician educates clients on the benefits of using recommended home-care products.

Contraindications : Sores or conditions that indicate the need or medical intervention contraindicate facials. Equipment that applies electricity on the skin should not be used on guests who have a pacemaker or metal plates, or who suffer from epilepsy, diabetes, or other conditions.

PEELS

The accumulation of dead skin gives skin a lifeless, ashy tone and uneven coloring. It interferes with the penetration of creams and serums into the living layers of the skin. The purpose of a peel is to slough dead skin off the epidermis. Peels unclog the hair follicles, and with regular use diminish the incidence of pustules, blackheads, and closed comedones. Postlaser resurfacing or dermabrasion, they help prevent milia and even the skin tone. They can reduce lines, wrinkles, hyperpingmentation due to sun damage or scarring and enlarged pores. Regular peels indirectly signal the dermis cell to increase cellular activity, which make peels an essential part of anti-aging programme.

Scrubs, also called *exfoliating grains,* are made of polyproylene, sand, or crushed seed of apricots or other plants. The finest ones are made with very small grains to avoid irrition to the skin. Some are formulated with sooting medicinal plants, such as calendula and are suitable for sensitive skin, acne or for use after medical peels. Scrubs get applied on wet skin with the fingertips or using a brush in a circular motion. Many scrubs are not suited for sensitive skin.

Peelings are made with kaolin and white clay in a creamy

substance that adheres to the skin. You can rub the peeling (which mixes with dead skin cells and impurities) off using your fingertips. Peeling are well suited for acne and skin.

Scrub and peelings are used during facials, and as home-care products.

Enzyme peels are usually made of plants like papaya or pineapple. They are used as part of a facial or treatment. These peels are in powder form, and are mixed with a toner at the time of use or dissolved in an aqueous solution. Some enzymes are formulated for all skin. The best formulations ease deep cleansing of the pores without side effects. Others may cause irritation in sensitive skin.

Alpha hydroxy acid (AHA) *and chemical peels* are another option. Milder AHA peels, such as glycolic acid when used in percentages ranging from 14 to 40%, get applied on the skin and then rinsed off within minutes, as part of a facial or as a separate service. They sting very little and there is no down time. The peels with low ph (2-2.5) and a high percentage of AHAs (30% and higher) work faster and deeper. The strongest AHA peels (those containing 75% glycolic acid, jessner, or non-resorcinol peels) are even deeper peels, causing the surface of the skin to turn brown and shed within about four days. The peels are done without pain reliever. Medical supervision or access is advisable with stronger peels.

Micodermabrasion is done with equipment that projects fine inert aluminum oxide crystals, or corundum powder, through a tube to the surface of the skin. The depth of the peel depends on the setting, the powder of the equipment, and the desired result. Light peels are an alternative to enzymes and AHAs. Deeper peels can improve scars, stretch marks, acne scars and discoloration. The quality of the crystals, the equipment, the skin-care products applied and experience all matter. There is no down time for mild peels and the discomfort is none to mild.

Contraindicatins : AHAs, chemical peels and micro-dermabrasion should not be administered on individuals using skin sensitizing medication, Retin A, or Accutane. Patch tests are advisable on sensitive skin.

MASKS

Besides the classical clay, kaolin cream or gel masks, hydrating and clarifying treatment masks can constitute a service by themselves or be part of a facial. Specialty masks can include an ampoule, the application of a gel (usually made of algae or even

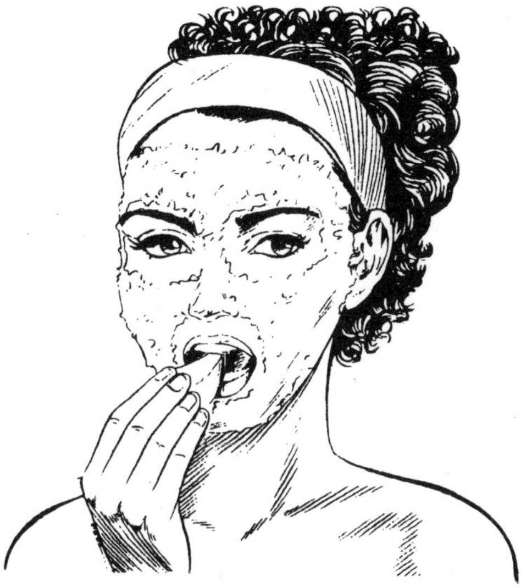

A claryfying treatment Mask

single-cell algae so nutrients can penetrate) and a setting solution to turn the mask into a film that can be lifted off the skin. Masks even skin tone, eliminate redness, and tighten pores. After a mask, the skin fells like silk. Less therapeutic results are achieved with masks that are "rubbery and occlusive," or waxy such as paraffin. Clay masks harden and get removed in one dramatic-looking piece. Rubbery and hardened clay masks mainly serve cosmetic pruposes, as they do not penetrate the skin with active ingredients, but just trap moisture in the stratum corneum.

Contraindications : Do not apply morks that harden on claustrophic individuals.

MANUAL LYMPH DRAINAGE (MLD) AND LYMPHOBIOLOGY

Manul lymph drainage (MLD) was developed by Dr. Emile Vodder in France in 1936. Dr. Vodder was seeking a therapeutic method of improving the health and quality of life of individuals suffering from fluid retention, toxicity, and various skin conditions. The method consists of a light massage that stimulates lymph circulation on the face or the body.

Lymphobiology is a proprietary science inspired by MLD; it uses equipment that produces the therapeutic massage of the manual method, but in less time, through glass tubes sliding on the skin. The equipment is classified as a therapeutic massager by the Food and Drug Administration (FDA). Information about the method has been published in medical journals following double-blind and single-blind medical studies (see "Noninvasive Techniques of Facial Rejuvenation," by Steven Bosniak, MD, and Marian Cantisano-Zilka, MD, Saunders, vol. 2, no. 4, Dec. 1999). Selected skin-care products with integral DNA are used as part of the Lymphobiology procedure to hydrate the tissues and supply nutrients at the cellular level. Lymphobiology cleanses the skin tissues of waste and toxins, and elmiminates swelling and dark circles, even after only one treatment. It naturally stimulates the immune system and lowers the sympathetic nervous system, including deep relaxation. Redness after extractions of comedones or after peels virtually disappears. Sagging skin tightens on the face and body. The treatments can be done in series or individually; they can be added to facials, body facials, hydrotherapy, and cellulite treatments. The clinical protocol recommends treatments before and after cosmetic surgery to eliminate bruising, swelling, and discomfort, to reduce stress, to prevent cellulite from coming back after liposuction and to improve elasticity.

Contraindications : Phlebitis, communicate with physician before and after surgery, and when medical conditions exist. Safe to use on individuals with pacemakers or metal plates since no electricity touches the skin.

❑ ❑

24

WATER IN EARLY MORNING

Water is panacea for chronic and incurable diseases. Rise early from bed. Do not wash your face and mouth as you do normally. Sit comfortably and drink four large glasses of water. Do not take any thing for 45 minutes. You can wash your face and brush your mouth after drinking water

Always drink water after an hour of breakfast and meals. Regular intake of water in early morning gives relief in following diseases:

- Diabetes
- Acne, Boils
- Headache
- Blood pressure
- Old age and wrinkles
- Arthritis
- Paralysis problem of ladies
- Anaemia
- Heart diseases, Faintness
- Cold, Cough, Asthma Bronchitis
- Obesity
- Meningitis
- Disorders of liver
- Tuberculosis
- Disorders of the eye

- Irregular menstruation
- Urinary problems, Stones etc.
- Hyperacidity, Asthma, Bronchitis
- Gastric trouble and diseases concerned with back, Spine
- Cancer of ovary
- Swelling, Fever
- Digestive disorders
- Piles
- Diseases caused by *Vata Pitta, Kapha*
- Mental weakness, etc.

If sick persons or soft natured persons with a delicate physique are unable to take four glasses of water at a stretch, they should start from one or two glasses and then gradually they should start taking four glasses. Take four glasses of water regularly. Experiments have proved that different diseases can be cured within the time given below by its regular use:

❑ Hypertension	Within one month
❑ Gastric trouble	Within ten days
❑ Cancer	Within six months
❑ Constipation	Within ten days
❑ Diabetes	Within one month
❑ TB	Within three months
❑ Leucorrhoea	Within one month
❑ Paralysis	Within three months

Other diseases described above may be cured within four to six months according to their nature. Drinking four glasses of water does not have any ill-effects on health. Only urge to pass urine will be great and you will pass urine in large quantities frequently. Passing of stool will be easy and complete. It will facilitate the expulsion of the accumulated waste matter very effectively and leave you fresh. Besides hydrotherapy certain other measures or house hold remedies are also advised for such disorders.

SOME IMPORTANT FACTS

- Never drink water before passing urine or just after passing urine.
- Passing urine after meals prevents formation of stones.
- Stand on forefoot and then pass urine. This posture prevents formation of stones.

- Water contained in copper vessel is hundred times more useful.
- Take juice of one lemon in a glass of warm water before going to bed. It gives relief in Coryza.
- Take juice of one lemon and tea spoon of honey in warm water in morning. It helps in curing obesity and improves complexion.
- In early morning, chew five leaves of Neem (Margosa) and Tulsi (Basil) and drink a glass of water after chewing these leaves. This can prevent you from carcinoma (Cancer) too.
- Take a little raw rice (one or two tea spoons) with a glass of water to cure liver disorders.
- The water kept in a Shankh (Conchshell) for a whole night is remedy for Stammering speech. Continue this for four to six months.

ROLE OF WATER ON STOMACH

There is secretion of stomachic juice in stomach to digest food. The more genuine the stomachic juice, the better digestion of food.

If someone takes liquid whether it is water, wine or beer, the stomachic juice will not remain genuine. It would be adulterated by the intake of water, wine or beer and would not be effective in digestion of food.

Similarly, if some person takes water six or eight times while taking his meal, it would liquidate stomachic juice so much that it would not be able to act as digestive juice.

Do not take water at all during meals. If you have to take it, take very small quantity of it, so that genuine stomachic juice may be absorbed in all eaten food.

If you feel thirsty after one hour or more of taking food, please take water in limited quantity. Body especially stomach needs water at interval from time to time to liquidate its juice, to increase its quantity and to absorb the solid material (food). The body itself informs whenever it needs it. Sometimes, the desire to take water is slow and sometimes it is very fast. One should be particular about intake whether it is from healthy or sick stomach. One should take it as much as it is sufficient and good for health.

It should be taken at equal intervals of time especially when one is suffering from fever. One should not take a glass of water at a stretch but each five or ten minutes in less quantity. Intake of water at a stretch by a patient of fever, will not quench his thirst, rather it would increase other symptoms of illness.

Water taken in less quantity is at once accepted and absorbed by stomach. Repetition of its intake at each half-an-hour produces juice in more quantity and removes whole dullness and constipation by flowing in body and intestines. It cools them also.

One can use lukewarm water or cold water according to its taste.

USE OF WATER

❑ Saline water is necessary in dehydration caused by cholera, fever, diabetes, diarrhoea, etc.

❑ It is useful to take water with salt, sugar, lemon and honey. Patients of kidney diseases should use water with salt in supervision of some naturopath.

❑ Some of vegetables, water of pulse, sharbat of lemon and juice etc. contain water. They give us minerals and salts along with water.

❑ ❑

25

THE ROYAL, CARNAL AND NOBLE FOOD WITH AROMATHERAPY

A well balanced diet contains sufficient quality of protein, carbohydrates, fats, salts and minerals. It is held in Yoga discipline that " as you eat, so you become,". This is because the kind and quality of food affects the physical as well as mental conditions of the individual. In Yoga all foods have been divided into three categories- Rajasi (Royal), Tamasi (Carnal) and Satvik (Noble). The Rajasi food comprises a variety of dishes. This type of food includes fried, roasted and fatty stuff, which is not desirable for

good health. A little intake of these types should be sufficient to titillate the palate. A little quantity of strongly spiced bitter or sour food (Tamasik) should also form part of diet which should mostly be made easily digestible, nourishing; and freshly prepared food which classifies the noble or Satvik food. Your food must give you the variety of all the six varieties of taste—sweet, salty, astringent, bitter, sour and biting. However, it is not only the quantity or quality of the food but your way of eating which is also very important. Whatever food you eat, masticate it thoroughly and allow the saliva to reduce the eaten morsel to a mere puop before gulpig it down. Always eat 75 to 80% of your total capacity and leave enough room for the movement of gas/ liquid etc. to help the system digest the eaten food quickly. Drining water with food should be totally forgotten. Drink water always half an hour before and half an hour after your having food. Drink enough of water between your meals but not with it.

For your help we are giving below some guidelines following which you shall remain healthy. Adherence to them will not only keep diseases and disorders at bay but enhance also the age of your healthy life.

❑ The food that we eat helps build the blood cells, nerves, bones and muscles in our body. It has been proved scientifically that food which is highly processed and high in protein, fat, salt and sugar leads to health problems. Nutritious food (balanced wholesome diet, moderate exercises, drinking enough water, that is 8/10 glasses (3 litres) of water, enjoying fresh air and sunshine, resting adequately every day, will ensure a healthy body and mind.

❑ Detoxify the system completely by fasting 2 to 4 days every three months with liquids, preferably fresh lemon water with honey 4-5 times daily and follow it up with an all fruit course for 5 to 7 days and then resort to normal diet. cautiously and gradually. Take enema on the days of fasting immediately after taking mud pack for 15-20 minutes. Also take abdominal pack at night.

❑ Abdoment must be kept cool and soft always. All liquid intake should be close to the body temperature as far as possible. Take mud pack, hip bath, enema and oil massage intermittently.

❑ Drink 1 or 2 glasses of water on rising, every morning.

❑ Dental health plays a vital role in curing a troubled abdomen. an unhealthy abdomen; an unhealthy abdomen is responsible for most of the dieseases.

❑ Use honey and molasses instead of sugar. Use a lot of garlic and some ginger if they suit. Take maximum roughage/fibre.

❑ Avoid non-vegetarian, concentrated, stimulating, intoxicating and gas forming foods.

❑ Ideal time for lunch is 10 a.m. and for dinner 7 p.m. May take some fruits (one variety only) around 2 p.m. Take only two meals a day and satisfy 80% of your hunger or appetite. Do not eat if not hungry or in bad mood/anger or at odd hours.

❑ Shun smoking, tea, coffee, alcohol, Zarda, Pan-maşala, soft drinks and drugs.

❑ Going for brisk walk and/or doing Yoga for 30 to 60 minutes daily is must.

❑ Wash vegetables and fruits properly under running water, scrubbing with a brush before cutting, as they contain pesticides and contaminates. If any germs are suspected then wash in water with diluted solution of potassium permanganate.

❑ Ensure good digestion,sound sleep, good appetite and evacuation of bladder and bowels regularly and naturally.

❑ Tension is very harmful, as it causes flatuence, constipation, irritability, besides liver and heart problems. Hence ,change the way of living. do not work for long hours. Do Shavasana and enjoy minimum 7 sound sleeps daily.

❑ Always use polyunsaturated oil and reduce salt and sugar intake to the minimum possible level.

❑ After lunch, rest a while and after dinner, walk a mile is a wise old recommendation. Relax in Vajrasana for 10-15 minutes afte the meal.

❑ Take very light but nutritious food which includes fruits, skimmed milk and yoghurt (curd).

❑ For healthy condition, 80 percent of alkaline foods to 20 percent alkaline diet is needed. Alkaline food and drink purify the blood . Refined and processed foods tend to acidify and pollute the blood and the cells.

Select your food from the following:

ACID PRODUCING FOODS

All fresh foods, fish, pulses, white bread, polished rice, white flour, nuts, confectionery, sweets, coffee, tea, alcohol, boiled buffalo milk, fried foods, concentrated foods, hydrogenated stuff, beans, onions peanuts, tomatoes, jam and all preservatives, pickles, unripe fruits, refined stuff, grapes and high protein foods.

ALKALI PRODUCING FOODS

All kinds of vegetables, potatoes, fresh fruits,butter milk, fresh lemon, coconuts, figs, dates, almonds, loquates, skimmed milk,yoghurt, molasses, sweet oranges, dry fruits, sprouts, whole flour/unpolished rice and honey.

❑❑

26

BEAUTY AROMA MASSAGE

Massage adds glaze to the skin and increases beauty. Regular massage stops premature aging and thus one remains young and energetic for a long time-When problems, diseases and other factors destroy the natural rhythm of the body and when it becomes dry, ugly, rough, heavy thin etc., certain types of massage can create miracles. If old men and women have 40 days massage every year, they look younger than their age. If one follows the instruction as to food, work, sleep etc., during add after 40 days massage, the old aging signs can be erased.

Beauty Aroma Massage

Massage for beauty starts from the base of the spine. If the spine is not in good shape, the figure of the person will not seem right and one's appearance is one of the most influencing factors in beauty.

After spine; the arms, forearms, palms and fingers are massaged. Then neck, shoulders and lastly the head and face are massaged. Milk cream, butter and special ubatan for skin texture are applied for massage. If skin of milk or pure cream is applied for massage. If skin of milk or pure cream is applied to any girl or boy of any age group, the effect can be seen within a fortnight. A week before the massage starts for beauty, the diet of the receiver should be fruits, vegetables, nuts, milk, cheese and cream. This diet should be continued not only during the massage but also for a week after the massage course is over.

Massage which consists, chiefly of friction is a doubly valuable aid to beauty. Not only has it the power to improve the condition of the skin and the complexion, but also to give lightness and grace to the whole physical form. Effleurage combined with kneading may form the main part. The effeurage stroke is long and fairly firm and is designed to mould the figure into lines of beauty. To remove stifflness or undue firmness of muscles kneading is necessary which removes all lumpy formation and mould the tissues into graceful lines. Effleurage must be followed by petrissage specially designed to remove imperfection.

The wrists, the ankles, fingers and toes and possibly the neck may be given suitable friction. The friction to the head should designed move the scalp and tapotement with the tips of the fingers is to stimulate the flow of blood.

Delicacy of touch is required not only in treating the face, but also the whole body. The whole series of movements should constitute one unified effort and the general effect should be soothing, pleasant and refreshing.

Women generally use different kinds of cream and talcum powders for beauty. But they have no idea that massage also brings beauty. They have no idea that massage with smooth hand with care, their face will shine like the moon. Kneading, stroking, vibration, clapping etc. may be applied. Knead the cheeks with the palms. For head massage anyone of the following oils can be used :

❑ Jeevanthyadi ❑ Triphaladi ❑ Baladatryadi ❑ Neelee-bringadi Kuntalakantbi ❑ Manjishtadi ❑ Eladi ❑ Asanae-ladi ❑ Bhringa-malakadi ❑ Kumkumadi ❑ Malathyadi ❑ Brahmi ❑ Nasarsha tailam

For the massage of the women's breast Yuvathyadi tailam is advised because that oil not only keeps the breast youth but also brings beauty. For massaging the waist including the sex organ and thigh of women Saubhagya Vardhana tailam may be used. At night while going to bed if the face is massaged with the cream of the milk adding lemon juice and turmeric powder the boils on the face and also small hairs will be disapperared.

For beauty massage about two hours are required. The time is distributed as follow :

Area of massage	*Duration of massage*	*Time to relax in corpse posture after the area massage*
1. Spine and Back	15 minutes	10 minutes
2. Hands and legs	30 minutes	10 minutes
3. Shoulder and neck	5 minutes	5 minutes
4. Face and head	30 minutes	15 minutes
Total time for beauty massage	80 minutes	40 minutes

After ubatan is removed from the body a raw milk massage or rose-water bath is adivsed for beauty. In winter sun bath after massage is marvellous. The hair should be washed with Ritha powder, Amala powder, Chickpea flour, yellow clay, goghurt, buttermikl or raw milk as suitable to the subject. During the beauty massage, once in a week more milk and fruit juice diet is essential.

Alcohol, tobacco, meat, fish, egg etc., are strictly prohibited during beauty-massage course.

❑❑

27

BENEFITS OF MASSAGE

Twelve benefits of massage are mentioned in the ancient book of Ayurveda. They are :

***Jarahar* (remover of old age) :** Daily massage to the spine, feet (soles) and heat with Almond oil increases virility and semen. The body is made of seven ingredients, such as :

1. *Rasa* (hormones, fluids, lymph)
2. *Rakta* (blood)
3. *Mamsa* (flesh)
4. *Medha* (tendons of nerves)
5. *Asthi* (bones, teeth, nails)
6. *Majja* (marrow)
7. *Shukra* (semen)

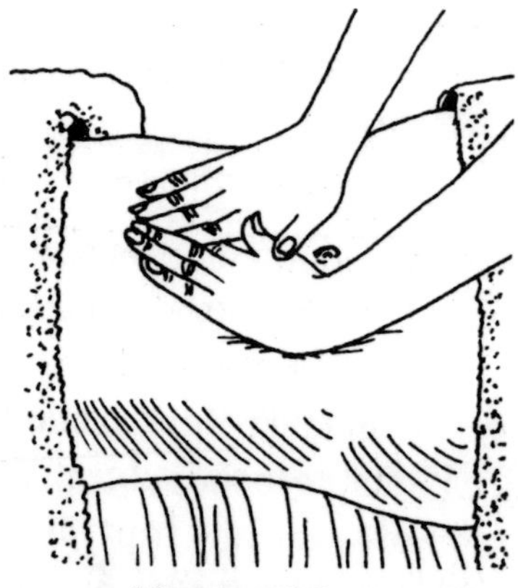

Massage of the stomach

Massage provides energy to all these seven ingredients and old age symptoms approach late.

***Shramahar* (Remover of Fatigue) :** By physical and mental strain one feels fat gue. It affects the muscles and causes tension. Rubbing, patting and squeezing muscles gently remove fatigue.

***Vatahar* (Remover of humour of wind) :** Rheumatism is one of the ailment caused by wind. Daily massage with Maha Narayana taila or other such Ayurvedic oils help to remove the troubles created by wind or gases.

***Darsanakar* (Increases sight) :** Regular massage improves sight and keeps blindness and other diseases of eyes away. Feet massage especially under the big toe and also massage of spine, neck and head will remove eye troubles and improve vision.

***Pushtikar* (Strengthener) :** By rubbing, pressing, kneading etc. the circulation of vital life fluids increases and makes the body strong.

***Ayushkar* (Supplier of longevity) :** By massage the longevity increases.

***Swapnakar* (That brings sleep) :** Massage induces sleep. Head and feet massage with pumpkin seed oil before going to bed gets the patient sleep.

***Twakdhritakar* (Skin strengthener) :** Massage makes the skin smooth, shining and strong. Dryness is the sign of disturbed wind element in the body.

Some times dryness comes by meditation, mental work, anxieties and worries. The people in cold regions get dry skin facing the chilled air.

***Klesha sahatwa* (Tolerate troubles) :** Resistance against disease and disharmony increases by massage because it excites production of antibodies and strengthen the above mentioned seven ingredients. The anti bodies give more resistance to disease and the strength of seven terms gives tolerance.

***Abhighat sahatwa* (Tolerate injuries) :** One who gets massage regularly recovers injuries more quickly than others who do not get massage.

***Kapha-Vata Nirodhaka* : (Protector from the tronbles of mucous and wind) :** Regular massage protects from the trouble of mucous and wind.

***Mrija Varna Baidprada* (Giver of colour and strength to skin) :** By massage the colour and the texture of the skin improves and hence it gets more strength. So Ayurvedic massage is highly praised by using oils.

❑❑

28

MARMA POINTS AND OILS

Marma points are energy centres of the body. Marma means secret, hidden and vital. The Chinese used *marma* points to develop the complex system of energy points known as the acupuncture meridian system. These points were used in ancient times to energetically harm the enemy by wounding or striking a blow at these vital spots. Physicians also studied these points in order to heal soldiers wounded in battle.

Know your Marma Points

Marma points are points of connection between the physical body and the subtle energetic bodies. They often relate to specific muscles, organs or tissues. *Marma* points can be used in self massage or massaging others in order to balance energies, restore normal function, energize or relax. *Marma* points are traditionally used in combination with Indian massage but can be used alone or with other methods.

Marma points are located on the body by taking finger measurements from various points. Because people have different size fingers, the patient's own fingers are used to measure. *marma* points are not as specific as acupuncture points, and in fact, can be as large as six inches across. For the purposes of this book, we have used a chart and written descriptions to help locate the points.

Traditionally, medicated oils were used to energize and massage these *marma* points. Here in the west, essential oils have been substituted as they are much more common and are in fact stronger and more potent than medicated oils. Because each *marma* point refers to an anatomical area or body function, specific essential oils will appropriately stimulate that part or function. In listing the *marma* points, we will give their number (our system), their Indian name, location, the body part or function to which they refer, and a few of the many essential oils associated with their stimulation.

Marma points are massaged with the thumb. A drop of warm oil is applied to the marma point before massage; this oil will be premixed with the appropriate vegetable and essential oils for the individual and the condition being back inward, slowly increasing pressure, outward, inward, in ever increasing and decreasing circles. Perform about five circles going out and five circles coming back; do this three times. *Marma* points which are blocked or our of balance will be more tender and painful than other marma points. If you suspect a marma point is blocked, you may add one drop of a specific essential oil for that marma point, right onto the area where you have already applied the general massage oil. This additional stimulation will energetically free up the point.

MARMA POINTS CHART

Indian Name	*Location*	*Function/area of Body Affected*	*Essential*	*Oils*
ARM				
1. Kshipra Thumb	Base of thumb	Passion Connection Stomach	Cardamon Sandwood	Fennel Carmina tives
Kshipra	Base of little finger	Passion Connection Stomach	Cardamon Sandalwood	Fennel Carmina tives
2. Talhridaya	Center of palm	Heart	Cardamon Rose	Orange
Talhridaya	Tips of Fingers	Nervousness Circulation	Sandalwood Champa	Rosewood Ylang Ylang
3. Manibandha	Thumb Side of Wrist	Expressing Yourself in the World	Vetiver Rosewood	Jatamansi Valerian
4. Koorchsha	Little Finger Side of Wrist	Circulation	Lavender Juniper Orange	Cypress Keawa
5. Karpooram	Middle Front of Elbow	Sexual Metabolism	Cinnamon Jatamansi	Clove Dhavana
6. Kurpara	Inside and Outside of Elbow	Right-Liver, Gall-bladder Left-Spleen	Ginger Myrtle Coriander	Rose Rosemary
7. Oorvi	Outer, Middle Arm	Blood Circulation	Thyme Camphor Clove	Eucalyptus Orange
NECK				
8. Kraknrik	One Inch Blow Base of Skull to Side of Spine	Heart Opening Lungs Chest Congestion	Cajeput Eucalyptus	Basil
9. Unnamed	Center Base of Skull	Mental Fatigue Allergies Myrtle	Rosemary Basil All Citrus	Lemon grass
10. Manya	Front of Neck Under Ear	Blood Vessels Circulation	Rosemary Lavender	Juniper Geranium
11. Siram -antrika	Lower Front of Neck	Mother of All Vessels	Myrtle Camphor Cypress	Eucalyptus Sandalwood Cajeput

Indian Name	*Location*	*Function/area of Body Affected*	*Essential*	*Oils*
CHEST				
12. Neela	Chestbone/ Collarbone Junction	Thyroid 5th Chakra	Seaweed Absolute	Cajeput Sandal-wood
13. Apast-amgh	Right Upper Chest Below Collar Bone	Muscle Tone Heart	Rosemary Cardamom	Lemon-grass Rose
14. Kaksh-adhara	Left Upper Chest Below Collar Bone	Muscle Tone Heart	Rosemary Cardamom	Lemon-grass Rose
15. Hridayam	Upper Central Chest	Thymus 4th Chakra	Yarrow Saffron Myrtle	Cumin Angelica Rose
b. Hridayam	Lower Central Chest	Heart	Cardamon Saffron	Rose Orange
16. Manipura	Lower Tip of Sternum	3rd Chakra Will	Sandalwood Dhavana	Anise/ Champa
ABDOMEN				
17. Nabi	2" Below Navel	Balance Creativity Elimination 2nd Chakra	Ginger Trifolia Cedarwood	Clary Sage Cypress
18. Vasth	On Central Public Bone	Sexual Energy Survival Sandalwood	Ginger Dhavana	Yarrow Trifolia
LEG (FRONT)				
19. Lohita-ksham	Groin-Ingu-inal Ligament	Lymph Drainage Ylang Ylang	Rose Nutmeg Champa	Geranium Jasmine
20. Oovi	Front Mid Thigh	Letting Go	Trifolia Yarrow	Lavender Rosewood
21. Ani	Central Above Knee	Balance	Yarrow Yarrow Lavender	Rose Sandal-wood
22. Janu	Two Points Above Knee	Balance	Sandalwood Cedarwood	Yarrow Lavender
b. Janu	Two Points Above Knee	Joints	Sandalwood Cedarwood	Yarrow Lavender
23. Unnamed	Mid Outside Shin	Kidney-Adrenal	Orange Cypress Myrtle	Cedarwood Sandalwood

Indian Name	*Location*	*Function/area of Body Affected*	*Essential*	*Oils*
24. Unnamed	Lower Inside Shin	Reproductive System	Dhavana Geranium Clary Sage	Angelica Vetiver
25. Gulpha	Inside and Outside Ankle	Reproductive System	Dhavana Clary Sage	Jatamansi Vetiver
FOOT				
26. Khipram	Above and Below Where Tose Join	Sinus Lymph	Rosemary Eucalyptus	Camphor
27. Koorcha	Ball of Foot	Stomach	Keawa	Sandal-wood
28. Talhri-dayam	Center of Foot	Heart	Rose Cardamon	Sandal-wood Rosemary
29. Koor-chshir	Center of Heel	Spinal Alignment 1st Chakra	Angelica Trifolia	Jatamansi Vetiver
LEG (BACK)				
30. Indravastih	Center of Calf	Cramps Leg Pain	Lavender Lemongrass	Winter green
b. Indra-vastih	Lower Calf	Athletic	Lavender Lemongrass	Winter green
31. Janu	Behind Knee	Spleen (Left) Liver/Gall Bladder (Right)	Angelica Lemon Balm	Lemon Yarrow
32. Aanih	Lower Back of Thigh	Intestines	Trifolia Ginger	Thyme
33. Vorvee	Upper Back of Thigh	Circulation of Leg	Juniper Cypress	Eucalyptus
34. Kteek-taninam	Center of Buttock	Equilibrium	Yarrow Lavender Sandalwood	Geranium Rose
BACK				
35. Gudam	Tip of Tail Bone	Alignment 1st Chakra	Vetiver Jatamansi Cypress	Labdanum Ginger
36. Kukun-daraye	Top of Sacrum	Alignment 2nd Chakra	Cypress Orange	Birch Juniper
37. Nitamba	Lower Kidney Area	Kindney	Lemongrass Juniper	Cypress Orange

Indian Name	*Location*	*Function/area of Body Affected*	*Essential*	*Oils*
38. Koopram	Upper Kidney Area	Adrenal	Angelica Lavender	Yarrow Geranium
39. Vrahti	Mid Back	Heart, Lungs	Rosemary Eucalyptus Cardamon	Camphor Rose
40. Asphalakah	Upper Back	Thymus, Heart	Thyme Yarrow	Lavender Rose
SHOULDER				
41. Asaha	Top of Shoulder	Relaxes Nervous system Self Esteem	Ginger Rosewood	Sandalwood Cedarwood
42. Shaunkh	Above and in Front of Ear	Clear Hearing	Lavender Eucalyptus	Peppermint
43. Utksh-epau	Above and Behind Ear	Increasing Awar-ness & Brain Activity	Basil Camphor	Rosemary
44. Apa	Temple	Vision	Peppermint Basil	Clary Sage Lemon
45. Sthapui	Between Eyebrows	Balancing 6th Chakra Pituitary Inner Vision	Lavender Jasmine Keawa	Camphor Basil Henna
46. Adhipati	Top of Head	Pineal Self Realization Balances 7th Chakra	Myrrh Shamama	Frank-incense
47. Nadi	Back Top of Head	Posterior Pituitary	Brahmi	Sandalwood

❑❑

29

AROMA-MASSAGE ACCORDING TO *DOSHA* TYPE

Each dosha type requires a different type of massage according to the qualities which are exhibited by the *dosha* imbalance.

VATA MASSAGE

Because *Vatas* are already dry, cold, irregular, and rough, they need to have a massage which is oily, warm, smooth and nurturing. Stroking should be firm, but smooth. Abrupt, rough movements can be irritable and disturbing to *Vata* types. Lots and lots of warm oil should be used. Excess oil can be allowed to sit on the

Tridosha Massage

skin (after you've worked on the area) to soak in; *Vata* bodies will just absorb it. Oil should be allowed to stand and soak into the tissue over the entire abdomen. Keep *Vatas* warm with sheets, heating pads, even blankets.

PITTA MASSAGE

Pittas are oily, hot, intense and fluid, so they need a massage which is calming and relaxing. They do not need as much oil as *Vata* types and their oils need to be of a cooling nature. The massage should be deep and varied, and the subject's mind can be kept occupied by using different techniques. *Pitta* tissues can sometimes be inflamed or irritated, so care should be used in these areas. Too much fast movement can worsen their imbalance; the massage needs to be slow and deliberate without a lot of movement from one area to another. *Pittas* can become irritable if the therapist is not centered.

KAPHA MASSAGE

Kaphas require the most vigorous type of massage to stimulate their sluggish metabolism and lack of fluid movement. Fast, even harsh, movements are appropriate, with as little oil as possible. If the *Kapha* is really out of balance, increasing amounts of diaphoretic an diuretic essential oils will be helpful. Since you will be using less oil, you can increase the mixture to approximately 75-100 drops of essential oil to four ounces of vegetable oil. During the massage, it's important to draw *Kaphas* into conversation so they can explore and let go of their own feelings, which they are usually reticent to divulge.

❑ ❑

30

ENVIRONMENTAL AROMA FRAGRANCING

Today we are very fortunate to have so many ways to disperse essential oils into the air. Aromatherapy rings rest on top of light bulbs, using that source of heat. There are electric diffusers which use aquarium pumps to force air and essential oils into a fine mist; however, in many of the aromatherapy diffusers, the aquarium pump makes a background noise which may be

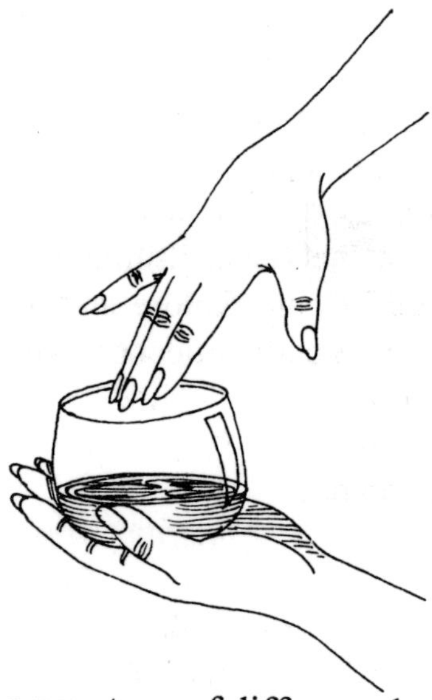

nnoying. There is a new type of diffuser whcih utilizes a cotton wick saturated with water and essential oils, and a silent fan which diffuses the oils into the room. With an aromatherapy lamp (potpourri pot), you can create magic just by lightinng a candle. You can bring the aromas of nature into your home all day.

When the children were small and they came home with colds, we would immediately light an aromatherapy lamp in their play room, using rosemary and eucalptus oils.

A vaporizer is a great way to diffuse oils and to put moisture and a wonderful aroma into a dry room. Just add 10-15 drops of oils into the water. If you burn a wood stove, place a pot of water on top and periodically add essential oils. In the winter, it is especially important to add moisture and oils to the dry, overheated air.

One of the fastest and easiest ways to environmentally fragrance a room is to use a spritzer of spray bottle. These are easy to obtain but unfortunately most of them do not contain components in their pump mechanism which can withstand essential oils, even in dilution. We have bought dozens of pretty plastic spray bottles in grocery and drug stores, only to have them fail, sometimes in a matter of days. For a bit more money, you can but a spray bottle which is resistant to chemicals. Try a garden shop. The intended use for these sprayers is for pesticides and herbicides, and they're not beautiful (with all kinds of information, warnings and technical information on them). However, you can spray-paint the bottles with your favorite color, or glue some pretty cloth or paper around outside. These will work with your ordinary dilutions of essential oils. In a quart of water, 15-30 drops is generally more than sufficient, and you'll be surprised how long that quart will last, and at the dramatic change in the environment. Plants love to be spritzed, and the essential oils in your spray bottle only add more life to them as long as your mixtures are well-diluted. Plants will be happy to take in the essential oil from one of their brothers and use it in their own defense and immune systems.

Some people use these sprays to encourage fleas to leave their pets, using mixtures that insects don't like—such as pennyroyal, sage, eucalyptus, tea tree, and citronella. I would recommend doing this outside, so that if the fleas jump off, they will not be jumping off in your house. Be sure to protect your pet's eyes from the spray.

You can drop a few drops of essential oils into the wax of a burning candle, and as the candle draws the oil up into it's wick, the essential oils will be released (the burning alters their smell somewhat). You can also do this with oil lamps.

It is possible to add essential oils to incense. Nag Champa, which is one of my favorite types of incense, is made from the bark of the champa tree. But you can add champa flower oil on to the incense before you light it. Other favorite incense additives would be sandalwood, camphor, jatamansi, rose and cinnamon.

The number of ways to add essential oils into the environment is only limited by our imagination. Sophisticated diffusion systems for industrial use have been developed, in which quantities of essential oils are diffused into air conditioning systems and circulated throughout whole buildings. These are being marketed and used around the world, especially in Japan. Increased work efficiency has been documented when workers are exposed to changing essential oil aromas every 15 to 20 minutes.

❑❑

31

AROMA MASSAGE DO'S & DONT'S

In basic terms massage is a way of stroking the body, with variations in the length and depth of strokes. However, you should always direct firm strokes towards the heart, as this will be beneficial to the circulation.

Long flowing massage strokes with little pressure on the body are the most soothing and relaxing. This type of movement is called *effleurage*. It is done with the whole hand using gentle, even pressure and is often used to start and finish a massage.

Patting or tapping the skin with your fingers quickly and slowly is stimulating and helps to increase blood flow. This is called tapotement. It is usually done on small areas such as the forehead, cheeks and neck.

Petrissage involves squeezing and releasing a muscle or part of a muscle group. A good example of this kind of movement is kneading dough. It is mostly done with both hands, particularly on the thighs and buttocks. Petrissage helps strengthen muscle fibre, remove waste products and ease fatigue.

There's another type of massage movement called friction which creates just that it involves rubbing the hands backwards and forwards across an area and is very warming and stimulating to the tissues. Rubbing our hands quickly together on a freezing winter day is a good example of how friction can work.

A professional aromatherapist uses mainly effleurage and works on pressure points with some frictions and petrissage, but there is no reason why you can't vary the movement if you decide you would like to try giving a simple massage.

You don't need to be an expert to give a soothing massage to family or friends. Once you've learned a few basic movements you'll probably be in demand.

DO'S AND DONT'S

Massage is a gentle healing art suitable for everyone from babies to the very elderly. However, there are certain times or conditions when it should be avoided (for example, when the person has just eaten a heavy meal). Often, this just means leaving out a body area but use your common sense and if unsure leave well done.

DO NOT MASSAGE

❑ Any infected area

❑ A person who is feverish or has a raised temperature.

❑ Over an area where varicose veins are present

❑ Over any unusual swelling or inflammation

❑ Bruised or broken skin

BEFORE MASSAGING DO

❑ Check with the person about to be massaged whether any of the above apply.

❑ Make sure the room is warm enough

❑ Warm your hands before massaging-cold hands are a real shock. Not a good way to begin!

❑❑

32

CREATING THE RIGHT ATMOSPHERE

Wouldn't it be wonderful to be massaged in a tropical country, with the warm sun beating down, soft sounds of the sea in the background and the sweet scents of flowers occasionally wafting over you?

Well, perhaps it's rather a far-fetched dream but it is still possible to create a lovely, relaxing atmosphere at home, especially with the help of aromatherapy oils. I think the most important consideration is that the room, or area, you use to give a massage is really warm. Believe me, there's nothing more shivering and

covered with goose pimples. Remember that while a person is lying still he or she generates less body heat: you know how difficult it is to get off to sleep if you feel really cold in bed.

It's a good idea to have a blanket, or large towel, so you can cover the parts of the body you are not working on. Also, it feels good to be wrapped up while being massaged. If you like, you can even wrap a hot water bottle in a towel and pop it under your patient's feet for a really luxurious treat.

Harsh, bright lights are unpleasant when being massaged. Obviously, until you feel confident in what you are doing you'll need a reasonalbe amount of light, just to see clearly as you go. A table lamp is sufficient for this: it gives a softer, gentler light than overhead lighting. Once you feel happy about your massage movements you can work by candlelight. The soft flickering of the flames has a soothing, hypnotic effect which is really relaxing.

Try to keep noise to the minimum, and close the curtains or blinds. This helps to cut out traffic noise. If you think you may be disturbed, unplug the telephone. It's now possible to buy some really interesting tapes to play in the background. Sounds of the sea, tinkling bells, birdsong and running water all combined with gentle, lulling music can take you off into a dreamlike state.

Part of the benefits of aromatherapy massage is the feeling of getting away from stressful day-to-day living, so music can be a great help in creating a relaxing atmosphere. This is a very personal thing and you'll find out for yourself which sounds are most relaxing for you. I find playing the tapes helps me to relax more while I am giving a massage, too, even when the day has been hectic and I am feeling less than calm.

Aromatherapy oils are marvellous for creating different atmospheres in the home and are much more authentic than using chemical copies or perfume sprays. Smells seem to strongly imprint themselves on our memories, and a certain aroma can evoke all sorts of feelings from the past. For example, the smell of warm spices, such a cinnamon and cloves, always reminds me of Christmasses spent at my grandparents'. And the sweet, sickly scent of benzoin reminds me of the day my little sister drank half a bottle of friar's balsam thinking it was some sort of chocolate drink!

There are several ways of scenting your home with essential oils. The simplest is probably to add a few drops of your chosen oil to a small bowl of water and then stand it over a radiator. The essentail oil floats on the water and gradually evaporates into the air, aided by the heat.

A more sophisticated method is to use an oil burner or vaporizer. These come in many different designs, but with the oil burners there is no need to use any water. You just put a few drops of essential oil into the top of the burner, then light a night light underneath. Vaporizers usually have a deeper dish into which you add water, followed by your favourite essential oil. However, whether you use an oil burner or a vaporizer, do be careful not to let it burn dry!

Used in this way to oils can become mood enhancers. They can remove stale smells or even help with conditions such as headaches, colds or insomnia.

Another way to perfume a room is to make your own pot-pourri. Gather flowers and herbs from your garden and hang them up in bundles to dry. (The airing cupboard is the ideal place for this.) Once dried, crumble them together, keeping some of the smaller flower heads intact. Now you are ready to perfume your pot-pourri with the essential oils of your choice. Generally, I find it better to use single essences rather than a blend.

Here are few suggestions:

Fresh and light : Lemon, coriander, vetivert and melissa

Warm and spicy : Benzoin, cinnamon, clove and patchouli

Sweet and flowery : Lavender, neroli, ylang-ylang sandalwood

You can also boost a tired pot-pourri by using aromatherapy oils in the same way.

Another way to perfume a room is with a light bulb ring. This is either a ceramic or metal ring which sits on a light bulb. Once the ring is in place all you do is pour in a few drops of essential oil. The fragrance is more effective when the light is turned on as the heat increases the oil's evaporation.

Now you have a few ideas on how to create a warm, relaxing atmosphere for aromatherapy massage we can look at the massage techniques in more detail. As I mentioned before, everyone can learn to give a simple massage; you'll be surprised at how enjoyable it can be.

❑ ❑

33

DIFFERENT WAYS OF USING ESSENTIAL OILS

As you are now well aware that how aroma therapy works over our body and environs. Now here are few ways to are different kinds of essential oils.

METHOD AND USAGE

Rub oil	:	8-10 drops of essential oil in 10 ml base oil. Use only 4-6 drops once a day preferably at night
Baths	:	6-8 drops in a tub, 2-3 drops in a bucket once a day

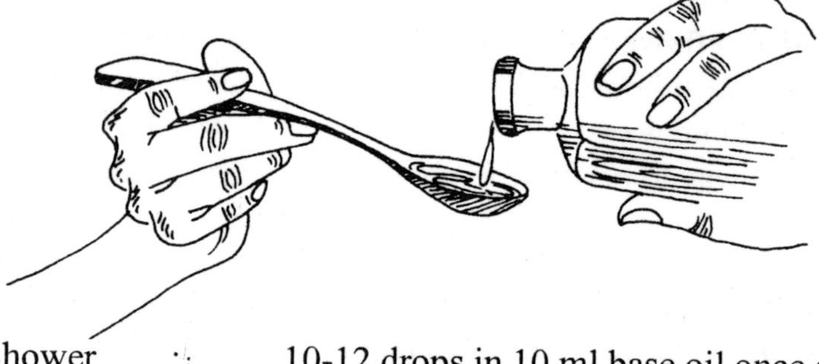

Shower	:	10-12 drops in 10 ml base oil once a day. Wash as usual. Add oil on your face towel, cloth or sponge or even your hands and rub briskly all over the body as you stand under the running shower. Breathe deeply to benefit from the aromatic vapour.
Massage oil	:	8-10 drops of essential oil for every 30 ml of vegetable base oil once a day

Diffuser	:	1-6 drops
Inhalation	:	2-3 drops once a day
Tissue	:	1-2 drops on a tissue. Sniff when required. Keep the tissue under the pillow during the night
Cotton balls	:	2-3 drops of essential oil on a piece of cotton and left for 10-15 minutes to dry. This piece of cotton can be kept in the cupboard, car, shoe rack, lockers etc.
Water bowls	:	1-9 drops of aroma oil to be added to bowl of boiling water. Keep in the room and close the windows, door and allow the aroma to spread in the room. This can also be used in the work places.
Room sprays	:	4-6 drops can be added to 30 ml of water in a spray bottle. Shake well and spray the mixture in the air. Avoid spraying directly on delicate machines. Ideal for home and office use.

CAREFUL HANDLING

❑ Essential oils are not recommended for internal consumption

❑ Certain oils are to be avoided during early pregnancy as they can induce menstruation and some even have diuretic properties which can deplete the fluid in the foetal sack. These oils include basil, clarysage, rosemary, juniper, marjoram, clove bud, fennel, cypress, peppermint, cedarwood. However this caution does not apply to oils used in vapourisers.

❑ Avoid exposure to sun for at least four hours after using essential oils as some oils can make the skin photosensitive to ultraviolet rays from the sun. Bergamot, lemon, orange, petitgrain are some such oils that can cause photo-sensitivity.

❑ People suffering from high blood pressure, epilepsy, neural disorders or kidney disease should avoid some oils *viz*. Black pepper, rosemary, cypress, juniper.

❑ Aroma oils are not a substitute for any drugs being taken under the advice of a qualified physician for serious ailments. It is always advisable to consult a qualified therapist before considering the use of essential oils particularly when suffering from serious ailments.

❑ Use the oils in recommended dosage. Usage in excess can lead to opposite effect to that which you are trying to achieve and there are chances of building up of the toxicity within the body. Ylang Ylang, marjoram, clarysage need to be used with utmost precaution.

❑ Essential oils should always be used diluted unless recommended otherwise.

❑ Keep out of reach of children

❑ Store the oils only in dark glass containers. The colour of the bottle should preferably be amber rather than cobalt blue. Only blended oils should be stored in cobalt blue bottles.

❑ Store in a cool, dark place away from sunlight to prolong the life of the aroma oils and also to preserve the therapeutic powers of the essential oils.

❑ Avoid using essential oils near the eyes or other sensitive areas.

❑ Avoid contact with plastic, varnished or painted surfaces.

❑ When blending essential oils use a stainless steel, glass or ceramic container and not plastic.

❑ Do not use essential oils on newborn. Use only one drop of lavender in the bath until the age of four months. For the use of essential oils on children up to the age of 12 years, all the essential oil dosage given to an adult must be divided into 4 portion.

❑ What suits one may not necessarily suit another person.

❑ Avoid certain aroma oils under the influence of alcohol. Oils *viz.* clarysage, marjoram, ylang ylang should particularly be avoided in case alcohol has been taken.

❑ Some oils may irritate the skin. Always do a skin patch test before applying the oils to larger area.

❑ If you are not sure of a particular blend, it is always better to take advise from a professional aromatherapist.

❑❑

34

EQUIPMENTS REQUIRED FOR MIXING OILS

After studying the feature, properties or category, select the essential oils you wish to mix and use. It is preferable not to mix more than three oils at a time for use. Also select the oils belonging to the same category. For example if you want to use more than one oil select them all from either floral, spicy, citrus, green or woody. Hence you could try out a mixture of perhaps lavenders, rose and ylang ylang as all these belong to the floral family.

Once you have selected the oils you want to mix and use, try the combination in a smaller quantity before you mix a large quantity so as to not waste the oils. Cut long strips of blotting paper, drop a drop each of the selected oils in case you wish to use equal amount of all the oils selected. In case you have decided to use any one or two of the selected oil more than the other, add two drops of those. Now hold the strip and move the oily tip of the blotting paper backward and forward under your nose as you inhale the aroma. Allow your sense of smell to be the judge and guide you in selecting the combinations.

Since aromatherapy is very personal you should get the other person to do a similar test before mixing a combination because it is not necessary that the mixture selected by you and liked by you should necessarily be liked by others too.

EQUIPMENT

❑ A 10 ml dark coloured glass bottles with stoppered caps for storing pure essential oils.

❑ Four eye-droppers or pipettes. You could use one only if you thoroughly wash it every time after every use.

❑ A small funnel for pouring carrier oils into bottles.

❑ A large, dark coloured glass, stoppered bottles for storing the combinations of oils or a ceramic bowl for immediate use. Please do not use metal containers or bowls.

❑ Strips of blotting paper.

❑❑❑